PCs made easy

STAGE 4

A PRACTICAL COURSE

Microsoft® Windows®
xp
edition

PCs made easy

easy

STAGE 4

A PRACTICAL COURSE

Microsoft® Windows®
xp
edition

PUBLISHED BY THE READER'S DIGEST ASSOCIATION LIMITED
LONDON NEW YORK SYDNEY MONTREAL

PCS MADE EASY
MICROSOFT® WINDOWS® XP EDITION
A PRACTICAL COURSE – STAGE 4

Published by the Reader's Digest Association Limited, 2003

The Reader's Digest Association Limited
11 Westferry Circus, Canary Wharf, London E14 4HE
www.readersdigest.co.uk

We are committed to both the quality of our products and the service we provide to
our customers, so please feel free to contact us on 08705 113366, or via our Web site
at www.readersdigest.co.uk
If you have any comments about the content of our books, you can
contact us at gbeditorial@readersdigest.co.uk

®Reader's Digest, The Reader's Digest and the Pegasus logo are registered trademarks
of The Reader's Digest Association Inc, of Pleasantville, New York, USA

For Reader's Digest
Project Editor: Caroline Boucher
Art Editor: Julie Bennett

Reader's Digest General Books
Editorial Director: Cortina Butler
Art Director: Nick Clark
Series Editor: Christine Noble

PCs made easy – Microsoft® Windows® XP Edition was fully updated for
Reader's Digest by De Agostini UK Ltd from *PCs made easy*, a book series created
and produced for Reader's Digest by De Agostini from material originally published
as the Partwork *Computer Success Plus*
The new edition was adapted by Craft Plus Publishing Ltd

© 2003 De Agostini UK Ltd

Printed and bound in the EEC by Arvato Iberia

ISBN 0 276 42755 6

CONTENTS

Windows®

Arranging your Desktop icons

It might seem trivial to worry about the state of your computer Desktop, but how you manage this important part of your PC can significantly affect the way you work.

It's easy to place what you want where you want it on the Desktop. We show you how over the next four pages.

In the office, an organized desk makes for a more efficient working environment. It's just the same on your computer, where a streamlined Desktop can make all the difference. As its name suggests, the Windows Desktop is the computerized equivalent of an office work desk. In itself it does nothing – it's merely a place where you can store all your useful equipment, work or even games.

● Close at hand

The number and type of icons that appear on the Desktop largely depend on whether your PC was upgraded to Windows XP or installed with it from scratch. However, in either case, the chances are that removing some unused icons and adding others will help you work more efficiently. What we'd all really like is a Desktop where the programs we need often are close at hand. With a well-organized desk you don't have to hunt through a successive

sequence of drawers, folders and envelopes just to find the stapler or calculator you need. In exactly the same way, a properly organized Windows Desktop will reduce the need for you to search through several layers of disk drives, menus, folders and files just to get to a program or file you want to use – especially when you need to use it quite often.

The key to making your Desktop work smarter and faster is to use shortcuts, and you can add a shortcut icon to your Desktop for any program. This is especially useful for accessing folders or

WINDOWS XP'S TIDY HABIT

From time to time, Windows XP suggests running the Desktop Cleanup Wizard. This program clears infrequently used Desktop icons into an Unused Desktop Shortcuts folder to help keep things tidy.

You can also start the Wizard yourself. Right-click on the Desktop and select Arrange Icons By from the pop-up menu that appears. Then select Run Desktop Cleanup Wizard, and you'll soon be tidied up.

programs such as My Computer, My Documents and Internet Explorer which may not have icons pre-installed on the Desktop with Windows XP. By adding a strip of program shortcuts to your Desktop you'll have simple and quick point-and-click access to them. Instead of browsing through folders in the Start menu you need only double-click on the program's Desktop shortcut to run it.

● The choice is yours

You needn't restrict yourself to making program shortcuts; you can also add shortcut icons for documents that you use frequently, such as a list of phone numbers, the novel you are working on or a simple 'to-do' list you've created in Notepad.

You can add as many document shortcuts as you have space for. If you don't want to clutter up your Desktop with a lot of document icons, you can create a folder for them (see Stage 1, pages 20–21). To access your document after that, you just need to double-click on the shortcut. Windows will automatically start up the program that created it with the document loaded and ready for you to start working on it.

● Advanced options

Once you have created Desktop shortcuts, you'll find that some new, powerful techniques will become available to you. For example, if you have created a shortcut for Microsoft Word, you can drag a text document onto it and Word will then launch and automatically open the file, ready for you to go to work on it.

Things get even better if you add a shortcut for your printer to the Desktop. When you drag and drop a document onto the printer shortcut, Windows will

immediately print it out. This means you don't have to start the program, open the document or use the File menu to print it. This can be very handy if you want to print something quickly, or if you'd like to print a number of documents at the same time.

To do so, you simply select a group of files with your mouse and drag them onto the printer shortcut as one. To select a group of files, hold down the [Shift] key and click on each of the files you want.

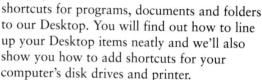

● Adding shortcuts

In the exercises that follow on the next two pages, we'll add shortcuts for programs, documents and folders to our Desktop. You will find out how to line up your Desktop items neatly and we'll also show you how to add shortcuts for your computer's disk drives and printer.

Choose the ones that suit you best and you'll be amazed just how much easier your Desktop – and therefore your entire computer – will be to use.

Creating a shortcut for Word

If you have a lot of software installed on your computer, your Start menu folders can become pretty congested. Here we make a shortcut for Word on the Desktop.

AS YOU load more and more software onto your computer, the Start menu's All Programs folder can become so large that Windows XP doesn't immediately show all of the items in the folder. This can make finding the program you want to start quite difficult. A simple way

around this problem is to create some program shortcuts on the Desktop. They will appear as icons that you can double-click on to start up the relevant program. For this step-by-step exercise, we'll create a shortcut for Word by copying it from the Start menu.

1 Click on the Start button and then click on the All Programs folder to reveal the list of software installed on your computer.

2 Locate the program you want to make a Desktop shortcut for – in this case we'll choose Microsoft Word. Using the right mouse button, click and drag the program entry onto a blank part of the Desktop.

3 Release the mouse button and Windows asks you what you want to do. Because the Word entry on the Start menu is already a shortcut to the Word program, it asks you if you want to move or copy the shortcut. Click on the Copy Here command.

4 A shortcut for Microsoft Word appears. You can move this icon around the Desktop, just like any other Desktop icon.

5 Look back at the Start menu's All Programs folder and you can see that the original Microsoft Word item is still in place. If you drag a program entry using the left mouse button instead of the right, Windows creates a shortcut but removes the original entry (this is useful if you want to make the menu shorter). Here we've dragged the Microsoft PowerPoint entry with the left mouse button and the program entry has been removed.

6 There's no limit to the number of shortcuts you can make for a program. If necessary, you can add a shortcut for Word – or any other program – to several folders. If you find that you're constantly working with a small number of folders, adding a shortcut for Word to each one might save you time.

7 Once you have created your preferred arrangement of icons, you can get rid of any shortcuts that are not needed. Just drag them to the Recycle Bin. Windows then asks you to confirm your actions (see PC Tips). Click on the Delete Shortcut button.

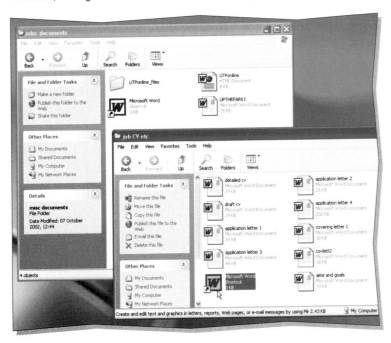

PC TIPS

Shortcuts and programs

Windows XP distinguishes the icons for programs from their shortcuts by adding the small arrow pointer to the bottom of shortcut icons. Ordinarily you would never alter the program file itself – it's tucked away in the Program Files folder on your hard disk. When you delete a shortcut, Windows reminds you that the program itself remains installed on your hard disk (see Step 7).

Adding extra shortcuts

You can also add shortcuts for your frequently used documents and your printer. This is a really good way of speeding up the opening and printing of documents.

1 Let's imagine that we have a to-do list that we keep as a simple Notepad file stored in the My Documents folder. We use it several times a day and it's too time-consuming to keep wading through various folders each time we want to open it.

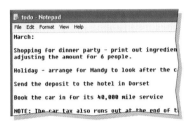

2 To add a shortcut to your Desktop for this document, open the My Documents folder and locate the 'todo' file.

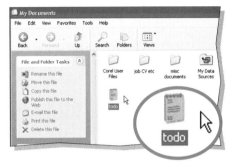

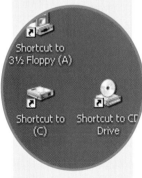
3 Use the right mouse button to drag and drop the 'todo' file from the panel on the right on to the Desktop. You will see an outline of the document appear as you drag it. Release it when it's roughly in position.

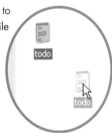

4 Windows asks you what you want to do. Select the Create Shortcuts Here option (we don't want to move the file, nor do we want to make an extra copy of it). A new icon for the document will appear on the Desktop.

5 If you don't want lots of document icons cluttering up your Desktop, you can create a folder for your various shortcuts. Click on the Desktop with the right mouse button, select New from the pop-up menu that appears and then click on Folder from the list of options.

6 A New Folder icon appears on the Desktop. You can give it a new name by typing one immediately while the title is highlighted. We've called our folder My Shortcuts. There's no arrow at the bottom of the icon because this is a new folder, not a shortcut to another folder.

7 This folder works just like any other folder; the only difference is that it's accessible direct from the Desktop. You can store files and document shortcuts in it. Drag the 'todo' shortcut icon from its position on the Desktop into the My Shortcuts folder.

8 Add as many shortcut icons as you like – even program and disk drive shortcuts – to your My Shortcuts folder. That way, all the Windows items you use most often are located in one place.

ADDING A PRINTER ICON TO THE DESKTOP

To add a shortcut for your printer to the Desktop, click on the Start button, select the Control Panel entry and then click on the Printers and Faxes icon in the Control Panel window.

A window will open that already includes an icon for your printer. Click on the printer icon and drag it onto the Desktop using the left mouse button. If the Desktop isn't visible, click on the Restore Down button near the top right corner of the Control Panel window.

Once the printer shortcut is on the Desktop, you need only drag a file or group of files onto the icon to print them out. Windows will do all the work for you, without requiring you to open the files separately.

Backing up important documents

If your computer were to fail, it's possible that you could lose vital information from your hard disk. But if you regularly back up important files, this needn't be such a disaster.

Things can, and do, go wrong with computers and, when crashes occur, hard disks can lose data. If this happens, it can prove impossible to retrieve some files and vital work may be lost.

Not only do you have to guard against computer error, but you also have to take into account possible human error. The Recycle Bin acts as a safety net to help prevent you from deleting files accidentally (Stage 2, pages 20–21), but it's still possible to overwrite files accidentally. For example, if you mistakenly delete text from a Word document, then save the file, the original text is lost. To avoid such accidents occurring, it is essential to keep copies of your important files. These copies are called back-ups. Keep them on floppy or Zip disks which can then be stored in a safe place.

● A good habit

It's good to try and get into a routine of backing up important files. If you regularly change a particular document, back it up as often as possible to ensure that you have an up-to-date version. One way to do this is to copy your documents to a floppy disk using Windows' normal drag and drop method (see Stage 1, pages 14–15). However, as you are likely to accumulate a lot of documents over a period of time, it is best to use a special back-up program. Windows comes with just such a tool, called the Backup or Restore Wizard. This keeps track of files and folders and backs them up automatically. It can also compress files so that they take up less space on the disks and it keeps track of information about the files should you need to restore them from the floppy disk.

● What should I back up?

There's a natural tendency to want to omit some files from your back-up routine. After all, the fewer and the smaller the documents that you back up, the quicker the process will be. However, an incomplete back-up is little better than not backing-up at all.

PC TIPS

Although it is wise to err on the cautious side when backing up, there is no need to back up your programs, such as Microsoft Word. These can be reinstalled straight from their original CD-ROMs, should the need ever arise.

In addition to the documents you create yourself, Windows suggests backing up important settings as well. For example, your carefully organized Desktop icons, colour scheme and Desktop background can be saved along with your documents. Although this type of data may at first seem trivial compared to the many documents you've put hours of effort into creating, it's surprising just how frustrating it is to have to set your PC up again from scratch.

Another example of data which often gets overlooked when you are making a back-up is Web browser Favorites. These are shortcuts to the dozens of Web sites that you may have bookmarked to make it easy to return to them. Few people can remember the addresses of more than a handful, so losing them is as annoying as losing a document. Similarly, the cookies that are stored on your PC from your

Internet sessions play an important role in your Web surfing. These tiny files are stored out of sight in a folder deep within Windows because there's never any need to open or edit them manually. On a typical PC there can be several hundred cookies. If a problem causes these files to be lost, you will find that many sites you have registered with no longer automatically recognize you when you return.

● Make it a habit

Whatever back-up choices you make, the secret of success is to think of backing up as a natural part of computing. If you can set aside regular sessions for backing up your files, and do it thoroughly, you will reduce the chances of losing your data. And by selecting the right type of back-up (see Back-up choices, below), you can minimize the chore.

WHAT IT MEANS

COOKIES

These are small files that your Web browser creates as you use the World Wide Web. Their purpose is to store small amounts of information about your preferences when you visit a Web site. For example, at their simplest, they let a Web site know if you have visited before.

Back-up choices

The Backup or Restore wizard allows you to choose the extent of each back-up operation, but you need to find an option that suits your back-up device and your own computing needs.

During the back-up process, the Backup or Restore Wizard asks you which files you want to back up. At the very least you should back up all documents that would be time-consuming or impossible to recreate.

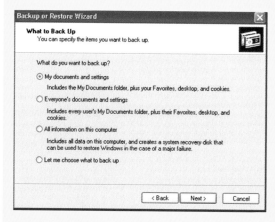

You'll quickly find that you can't back up many files to a floppy disk. If you're looking to back up regularly, it may be worth investing in a tape drive, such as that shown above, or in a Zip drive with high-storage disks.

There are a number of ways to begin the back-up process. For example, you can select the 'Let me choose what to back up' option and then choose individual folders and files. This approach may be the most realistic option if you don't have a CD writer or Zip drive attached to your computer and therefore have to back up using the floppy disk drive. However, unless you are very well organized with an encyclopaedic knowledge of all the files you have created, you may well forget important documents. It's also very difficult to make a rigorous back-up onto floppy disks as each disk can only store 1.44MB of data.

For most people, the best back-up option is 'My documents and settings'. Alternatively, if you share your computer with other people and need to back up their files too, you should choose 'Everyone's documents and settings'. However, both of these options need a device with a much bigger storage capacity than a floppy disk. A Zip drive – the latest version of which can store 750MB on a single disk – is one of the most cost-effective and efficient solutions.

The most complete – and therefore the most time-consuming – back-up option is 'All information on this computer'. This is only a realistic proposition if you have a high-capacity tape drive. These can store 20GB or more – equivalent to well over 10,000 floppy disks.

Using the back-up tool

Here's how to back up information contained in the My Documents folder on the hard disk to a floppy.

1 To access the Backup program, select All Programs from the Start menu, then Accessories, followed by System Tools. Click on the Backup entry.

If the Backup program isn't present on your PC, click on Control Panel in the Start menu, then the Add or Remove Programs icon. You can use the Add/Remove Components button on the window that appears to select the Backup program and install it from the Windows XP CD.

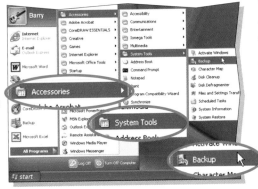

2 The Backup or Restore Wizard appears. Although there is an Advanced mode, it's best just to use the Wizard by clicking on the Next button.

3 The Wizard handles both Backup and Restore processes. The Restore process is shown opposite, but until you have made a back-up, there's nothing to restore, so make sure the Back up files and settings option is selected before clicking on the Next button.

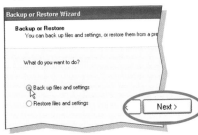

4 You then tell the Wizard which files and settings to back up (see Back-up choices, page 13). For most home users, the My documents and settings option is the most appropriate. Select your choice and then click on the Next button to proceed.

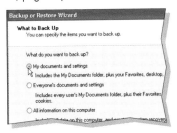

5 Now you must choose a name and destination for the back-up file. In this example, we have chosen the floppy drive, but you can choose any device on your PC – such as a Zip or tape drive. Type a name for this back-up into the bottom box and click on the Next button.

6 The final screen of the Wizard summarizes the choices you have made. If you want to change one of the settings listed, click on the Back button to return to the relevant screen. Otherwise insert a disk or tape and click on the Finish button.

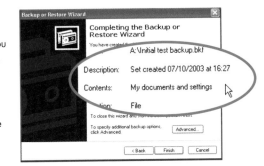

7 You must be patient while the back-up process starts and copies files to the disk or tape; the Backup Progress window shows how the copying process is proceeding. It's not advisable to start other programs until the process is finished – this allows Windows to concentrate on this task.

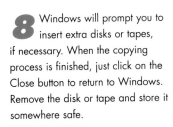

8 Windows will prompt you to insert extra disks or tapes, if necessary. When the copying process is finished, just click on the Close button to return to Windows. Remove the disk or tape and store it somewhere safe.

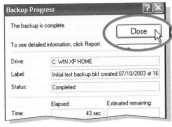

ADVANCED OPTIONS

Just before starting the back-up process, the Backup or Restore Wizard provides some important options that you can alter by clicking on the Advanced button in the final screen of the Wizard (see Step 6). Click on this and a screen will appear offering several types of back-up. The Normal back-up is the default and suits most casual home users, but the others can be useful. For example, an Incremental back-up only backs up those files that have changed since you last backed up. This is quicker and saves space.

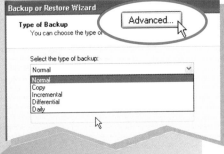

Restoring files from a back-up

The worst time to learn about restoring files is when something's actually gone wrong and you're in a panic, so it's a good idea to practise with a test restore so you are prepared for the worst.

1 Insert the floppy disk you want to use as a back-up and then start the Backup or Restore Wizard. Click on Next on the opening screens until you get to the page that includes the Restore files and settings option. Select this and click on the Next button.

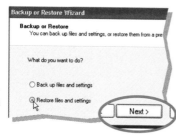

2 The What to Restore screen allows you to choose the files and settings you want to restore. In this example, there are two listed on the right of the screen. Double-click on the back-up file you want to restore.

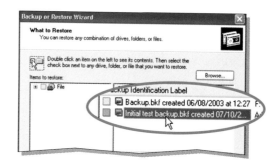

3 Both panels change to reveal the original location of the backed-up files – in this example, telling us the files were stored on the C: drive (the computer's hard disk). To restore all the files from that back-up session – perhaps you backed up a whole folder and have since accidentally deleted the folder – tick the box next to the C: drive on the right of the screen.

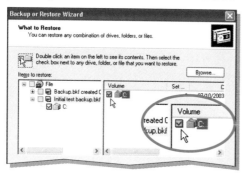

4 If, however, you want to restore a single file that you have lost or that has been corrupted, double-click on the C: entry and the lists expand. The panel on the left shows the folders and the panel on the right shows the contents of the current folder.

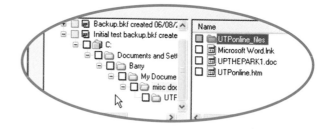

5 Select a file by placing a tick next to it in the list of files on the right. Click on the Next button.

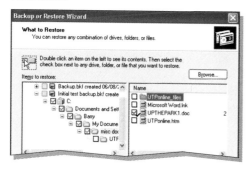

6 The final screen of the Wizard summarizes your choices. The default action is to restore the files to their original location, but you can change this if necessary (see PC Tips, right). Click on the Finish button.

7 The program now opens the file on the floppy disk and restores all or part of it depending on your choices. When it has finished, the Restore Progress dialog box displays a 'The restore is complete' message. At the bottom of the dialog box, the number and size of the files restored is shown.

8 Now open the folder that you originally backed up and look for the file that you chose to restore. In this example, we selected the UPTHEPARK1 Word document in Step 5 and it has been restored to its original folder, ready to use just like any other document.

PC TIPS

Although you'll often want to restore files to their original location, the Backup or Restore Wizard lets you alter the destination. This is useful when you want to restore an old document to compare it to a newer version.

To do this, just click on the Advanced button in the final screen of the Wizard (see Step 6) and choose an Alternate location.

Using the Startup folder

To make your computer load the programs you need to use as soon as you turn it on, just add shortcuts to the Startup menu.

I f you upgraded your PC to Windows XP from a previous version of Windows, you may have noticed a Startup folder within the Start menu's All Programs folder. Even if you bought a PC with Windows XP already installed, you can still switch this very useful folder on (see opposite). It can be opened and used just like any other folder, but Startup has a special function: any program placed within it will automatically run whenever the computer boots up.

This function allows your favourite programs to start automatically each time you switch on the computer. Just put a shortcut to the program into this folder and it will be ready and waiting for you as soon as the PC is switched on.

In every other way, the Startup folder behaves like any other folder; you can add or remove items by dragging and dropping them with the mouse (see opposite). However, you should not try to delete other items in the folder because Windows may need them.

● What you might find

Click on the Start menu, then All Programs and then select Startup. You might find that it already contains some items. Don't worry if you don't recognize them – some programs place items in this folder as part of their installation process, and these items are often required in order for the programs to work properly.

A few graphics cards also include special utilities that they install in the Startup folder. Although it's possible to remove these items, it's safest to leave them in place.

● Adding your own programs

It's easy to add your own program shortcuts to the folder. Once you have done so, these shortcuts will enable the associated programs to start up at the same time as Windows. This can be handy if you regularly use a single program, such as Word or Excel. But be

The Startup menu might already contain a few programs that Microsoft Office uses, so don't delete them.

careful: the more items you put in the Startup folder, the longer Windows takes to load, so stick to the programs that you most often use.

There's another very good use for this folder. If you place a shortcut to a document in the Startup folder, the program that created it will start with the document automatically opened and ready for you to work on. For example, imagine your simple 'to do' list created in Notepad (see Page 11). It would be useful to have your list appear when you start your PC. If you place a shortcut for this file in the Startup folder whenever Windows restarts, your list will pop up as a reminder.

You can check which programs are already in your Startup folder by calling it up from the All Programs folder.

WHAT IT MEANS

BOOT UP

The term 'boot up' refers to the process that commences when you switch on your computer. Before Windows or any other program starts up, the computer runs its own tiny built-in program to check whether crucial components are working correctly. After the computer boots up, it will load Windows and then you can begin work.

Adding a program to Startup

In this exercise we'll show you how to place the Calculator program in the Startup folder so that it opens automatically every time Windows starts up.

1 Click on the Start menu and then click on All Programs. This expands to reveal several folders and programs installed on your PC. If the Startup folder isn't in the list, you must switch it on. If it is listed (inset), you can skip to Step 5.

2 To switch on the Startup folder, it's first necessary to change to a different style of Start menu – one that looks like that on earlier versions of Windows (you can reverse the change later if you decide you prefer the Windows XP style, by reselecting the original option, see Step 3). First, right-click on the Start button and select Properties from the pop-up menu.

3 In the Taskbar and Start Menu Properties dialog box, select the Classic Start menu option at the bottom of the Start Menu tab. Click on the OK button.

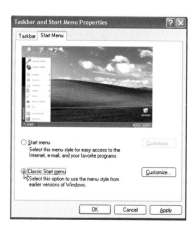

4 Click on the Start button once more. The Start menu is shorter, and your software folders are now listed under the Programs folder. The Startup folder – initially empty – appears in this list.

5 Now you can add items to this folder, by dragging entries from other folders in the Start menu into the Startup folder (see Stage 2, page 14–17). In this instance we are dragging the Calculator entry from the Accessories folder to the Startup folder.

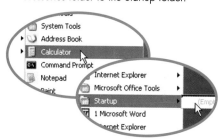

6 Before releasing the mouse button to drop it in the Startup folder, press and hold down the [Ctrl] key. A small + sign appears, indicating that Windows will copy the entry – leaving the original Calculator entry in the Accessories folder (see Move or copy, below). Release the mouse button and then the [Ctrl] key.

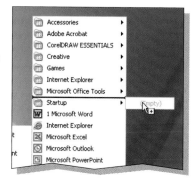

7 Now restart your computer by clicking on the Start button, then Turn Off Computer and then clicking on the Restart button.

8 Each time Windows loads, the Calculator program will appear on the Desktop immediately. If you change your mind in the future, you can remove the program from the Startup folder by right-clicking on the folder and selecting Delete from the pop-up menu.

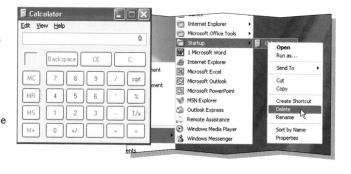

MOVE OR COPY

When you drag items to the Startup folder, Windows normally moves them from their original location. However, many people find this confusing when they later try to find the item in its original place. This is especially the case if you share the computer with other people in your family. Copy the file and Windows will then create an extra entry, avoiding any confusion.

The Program Compatibility Wizard

If you have older software that won't run on Windows XP, try the Program Compatibility Wizard to get it working.

Much software is written to run on any version of Windows, and works perfectly with Windows XP. However, some programs won't work at all with Windows XP, and others will need to be set up to work with it. The reason is that Windows XP was designed to be more reliable and less prone to crashing than earlier versions. In order to achieve this, Windows XP keeps a close watch on every program you install, and if it spots anything that could cause a crash, it stops the program.

● Good and bad

The good news is that the promise of better reliability is achieved, and you should find that your PC doesn't crash. The bad news is that some programs – the biggest troublemakers being games written for Windows 95 or 98 – are unable to work with this latest version of Windows.

You may find that games bought from the bargain bins of computer dealers won't run, or old demo versions of software downloaded from the Internet fail to install. Games are especially prone to this because they are often written to extract the maximum possible performance from your PC and, to achieve this, the programmers may not abide strictly by the rules.

On Windows 95, 98 or Me, the program may get away with minor irregularities and it won't affect the performance. However, if the same program is installed on a computer running Windows XP, it is halted before it has a chance to cause any problems. It might not always be Windows XP that stops the program from running: it's also possible that the program was written to run on an older version of Windows. Depending on the programming, it may fail to find its way around in the Windows XP environment.

● Help from a wizard

Microsoft was aware of the problems that its stricter XP regime could produce, and began a comprehensive software compatibility testing regime – you'll see 'Windows XP compatible' logos on an increasing number of new games and programs. For older software which won't run on Windows XP, however, you can try the Program Compatibility Wizard.

This Wizard leads you through a process that allows some subtle changes to be made to the way the program runs. For example, if your software was designed for Windows 95 or 98, you may be able to fool the program into thinking it's running on an older version of Windows.

Once you've run through the simple wizard procedure, you can test the program and, if it works, you can then save the settings. This means that every time you start the program, Windows makes the necessary changes for the program to run. The Program Compatibility Wizard won't be able to solve all problems with older software, but it's well worth trying as a first step.

Some older programs cannot work under Windows XP and produce error messages when you try to start them.

Making older software work on Windows XP

In this exercise we show you how to run the Program Compatibility Wizard. This wizard attempts to fool Windows XP in order to make a Windows 95 program run.

1 We're trying to run some software written for Windows 95 but it displays an error message when we try to install it on newer operating systems. Click on the Start menu, then All Programs and then Accessories. Select Program Compatibility Wizard from the menu.

2 The Wizard starts; click on the Next button on the opening screen, and then select the location of the program. In our example, the program is on the CD, so we have selected the second option. If the program is already installed on your computer, use one of the other options (see PC Tips, below). Click on the Next button.

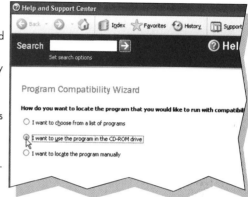

3 Now choose the version of Windows that the program was originally written for. In the case of games, it's often Windows 95, but check the software packaging. Click on the Next button.

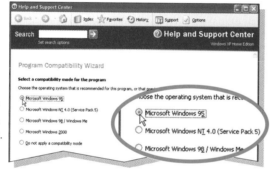

4 Windows XP displays data on the screen in a different way to previous versions of Windows. The Wizard allows you to alter three settings to match the environment the program expects. The program's manual can help you select the appropriate choices.

5 The next screen summarizes your choices. Click on the Next button and Windows XP starts the program with these settings. In this example, the program has been successfully fooled into working with Windows XP.

6 The Wizard asks if the program worked correctly, and if you want to save these settings. Click on the Yes option. You can also opt to send a summary of the settings to Microsoft to help it improve program compatibility.

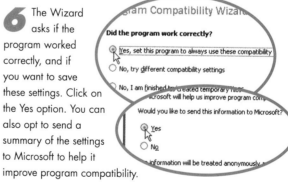

PC TIPS

If the problem software is already installed on your computer, you have two options for selecting it (see Step 2). The first option – 'I want to choose from a list of programs' – prompts Windows to list programs on your PC. This is usually the best option, but it can overlook programs. If this happens, click on the Back button and select the last option: 'I want to locate the program manually'.

INSTALL THE SOFTWARE

If the Program Compatibility Wizard cannot solve your software problem, there are some other steps you can take:
- Visit the software company's Web site for advice on running programs on Windows XP. Look for a Support or Help section.
- Visit the Web site of your graphics card manufacturer. Some software problems, particularly in games, are due to bugs in the graphics card software; a new download may be available that fixes the bugs when the program runs on Windows XP.
- If you have just bought the software, take it back to the dealer and explain that it doesn't work on your PC. You may be able to get a refund or exchange.

Dial-up networking

Windows' dial-up networking provides a quick and easy method of connecting to the Internet that works with any software.

Dial-up networking is one of the most useful components of Windows. It allows anyone with a modem to gain access to shared information on another computer. You can use dial-up networking to make a connection to any computer as long as the computer you are dialling is set up to receive incoming calls. The Internet is the classic example of a network you access by dialling, via an Internet service provider. In fact, the dial-up networking tool – as far as home users are concerned – is primarily used to provide a quick and easy connection to the Internet.

● Linking to the Internet

When you first open an account with an Internet service provider (ISP), you'll be provided with all the information you need to connect to the Internet. In some cases, primarily with content-driven ISPs such as AOL, you will also be given some specific software that connects you to the Internet and allows you to use email and the Web.

Although a few online companies and games producers continue to include their own proprietary connection software, this approach is increasingly uncommon. Instead, dial-up networking provides a more generic approach to connecting computers. The idea is that any program on your PC can ask Windows to open an Internet connection, without dictating which connection is used.

● Generic advantages

There are several advantages to this method. For one, it means that the software companies no longer have to write their own connectivity software. They can rely on Windows' own tried-and-tested dial-up networking software to handle the connection. This in turn means that there's a much smaller chance of software incompatibility or bugs causing problems when you connect.

Dial-up networking is a generic method for connecting to another PC or the Internet over the telephone line.

● Multiple connections

Windows' dial-up networking also allows you to create multiple connections. While many people are perfectly happy having one connection – the one automatically installed by their ISP – having a couple of extra connections can come in handy. For example, if your ISP's computers crash, you may find that you can't log on. If you only have one connection, this would mean that you wouldn't be able to use the Internet at all.

However, if you have several connections, it doesn't matter if one connection isn't available – you can just try another. Your Internet software works independently of the connection software, so your Web browser and email program will work as normal. Multiple connections are especially useful for connecting at busy times – if you hear the engaged tone, just try another connection. You are also able to choose the most cost-effective connection at different times of the day.

To add extra dial-up connections you will need to sign up with extra ISPs (see Accounts and connections, opposite) – it's a very straightforward process that will then put you in control of choosing which connection you want to use and when.

TWO WAYS TO CONNECT

With some ISPs, such as AOL, a dial-up networking connection is installed with their proprietary software when you set up your account. Although connecting to the Internet via these ISPs is normally achieved through this software, you can also connect by selecting the relevant connection from the Start menu's Connect To sub-menu.

By entering just a few details – most importantly the telephone number to be dialled by the modem – you create an Internet connection that can be used at any time by simply double-clicking on its shortcut. You can even tell the software to remember your user name and password so that you don't have to type it in every time (or you can choose not to do this if you'd prefer to limit the Internet access of other users of your PC).

● **Connection settings**
In addition to the basic information required for every dial-up connection – the ISP's telephone number, your user name and password – there are several other settings that are often overlooked but are well worth modifying to suit your needs.

For example, by opening the Network Connections window you can check and, if you need to, alter the settings for each of your dial-up connections. This is especially useful when you change ISP, for example. Instead of having to select your new ISP each time you try to connect, you can set one as a default. You can also delete your old ISP if you have closed your account altogether.

● **Other types of connection**
Windows XP handles all types of computer-to-computer connections in a single window and its New Connection Wizard allows you to add several different types of connection. Here, we focus on dial-up Internet connections, but in future volumes we'll also look at home networking connections.

Accounts and connections

For most home users, each dial-up networking connection is based on an account with an Internet service provider.

SIGNING UP with an Internet service provider (ISP) is a three-part process: choosing a tariff, agreeing to the terms and conditions of the service and then setting up the software so that Windows can create a connection to the ISP whenever you want. Often, an ISP creates a CD-ROM to handle the whole process (see Stage 1, pages 146–149). However, once you have signed up with an ISP and installed its software, you can visit the Web sites of other ISPs and sign up for other accounts online – there are no restrictions.

In an ideal world, you'd never need to do this, but every ISP's computers suffer from crashes and their connections to the rest of the Internet can also suffer from outages. In this case, having a back-up connection is perfect. You can search for an ISP and sign up with the one which offers a tariff that best suits your needs. A service which has no monthly fee and only charges for the time you are connected is perfect for a back-up connection, for instance.

Some online sign-up processes automatically download the new connection details to your computer – if so, a new icon appears in the Network Connections window automatically (see inset, below right). If not, you can create a new dial-up connection manually (see page 22). This will only take you a couple of minutes, so don't be put off signing with your preferred provider.

To sign up with an extra ISP online, visit its Web site and follow the Join or Sign Up links – they'll usually be clearly displayed on the home page.

Choose a tariff that doesn't commit you to unnecessary expense, such as regular fees, as you won't be using the ISP on a frequent basis.

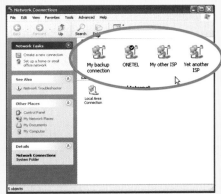

Each ISP account adds an extra icon to the Network Connections window – you can choose to use any connection at any time.

Setting up a new dial-up connection

Here we show you how to establish a dial-up networking connection to an Internet service provider's computer. When completed, you'll have a back-up connection to the Internet.

1 Sign up for an ISP account (see Accounts and connections box, page 21). Click on the Start menu and then on Connect To. A small sub-menu appears with your existing ISP connection at the top of the sub-menu. Select Show all connections.

2 The Network Connections window is divided into two parts. At the top is the icon for your ISP connection, under the Dial-up heading. (If you have a broadband connection or if you have a network of PCs at home, you will also see icons in the centre of the window.) Click on the Create a new connection link in the Network Tasks panel on the left of the window.

3 The New Connection Wizard guides you through the process. Click on the Next button on the first screen and then select the type of connection on the next screen. For dial-up connections, select the Connect to the Internet option and then click on Next.

4 As you have signed up online, you have the information you need to create a connection for this ISP, so select the Set up my connection manually option and click on the Next button. On the next screen, choose the Connect using a dial-up modem option and click on Next.

5 On the next screen type in a name for this connection and click on Next. Then type in the phone number for the connection. Click on the Next button.

6 Type in your user name and password for this ISP connection. Then choose which of the three options you want switched on. For a back-up connection, it's best to turn the first two options off. However, you should leave the **firewall** option ticked. Click on the Next button.

7 That's all you need to do. Click on the Finish button to close the Wizard. Now you can choose which connection to use whenever you connect to the Internet.

WHAT IT MEANS

FIREWALL

This is an excellent security feature for Internet computers that's built into Windows XP. When your computer is connected to the Internet, it is visible to every other computer on the Internet – including those used by hackers. A firewall is a software barrier that makes it almost impossible for hackers to gain access to your PC.

Checking dial-up connection settings

Use the Network Connections window to check and, if necessary, alter the settings for each of your dial-up connections.

1 Open the Network Connections window by clicking on the Start button, then Connect To and then Show all connections. The status of each connection is indicated by its icon. In this example, the My backup connection icon has a red cross on the cable which means it isn't available.

2 To correct the problem, click on the icon and read the Details panel on the left of the window where a status summary is given. In this example, it reports that the connection is unavailable because a device – the modem used for the dial-up connection – was switched off when the ISP connection was first set up.

PC TIPS

If you close an account with an ISP and want to stop using it, right-click on its icon in the Network Connections window. Select Delete from the pop-up menu to remove it from your computer. Before deleting it permanently though, make sure that the connection to your new ISP is working.

3 Getting the connection working is simple. Shut down the PC, switch on the modem and restart the PC so that Windows XP detects it during its start-up process. Open the Network Connections window again and you'll see that the red cross has disappeared from the icon and the connection is working.

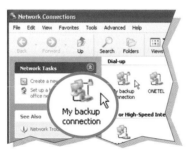

4 However, there's still a small box on the cable of this icon which isn't present on our other connection. Right-click on the other connection and select Properties from the pop-up menu.

5 When the Properties dialog box for this connection appears, click on the Advanced tab. As you can see, this connection does not use Windows XP's Internet Connection Firewall (see page 22). Tick this box.

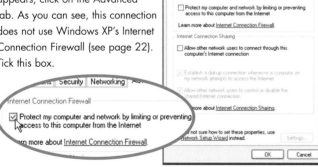

6 The firewall is the only advanced setting that you should consider changing – the others are best left alone. However, click on the Options tab and you can alter some of the more basic aspects of the connection, such as the amount of idle time before Windows disconnects your computer from the Internet. Reducing this setting will help minimize your phone bill should you forget to disconnect.

7 Click on the OK button to return to the Network Connections window. Notice that the firewall now appears as a barrier on this cable, too.

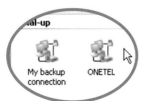

8 Finally, choose which of your dial-up connections to make the default, so that Windows automatically chooses it (unless you specify another connection). To do this, right-click on one of the connection icons and select Set as Default Connection from the pop-up menu. Windows adds a small tick to the icon to indicate its default status.

STAY CONNECTED

Even if your main ISP connection is working perfectly, remember to connect to the Internet with each of your back-up connections from time to time. This is necessary because some ISPs will cancel your account if it remains unused for a prolonged period of time – check the terms and conditions when you sign up.

Introducing Windows Media Player

The Windows Media Player acts as a Multimedia centre, playing music CDs as well as sound and video clips, accompanied by some dazzling light effects.

The CD-ROM drive is actually misnamed – it isn't specific to computer CDs at all and the hardware and electronics are identical to those in most hi-fi CD players. As a result, normal music CDs can be played as easily through your computer speakers as through your hi-fi system. The only real electronic differences between CD-ROM players and hi-fi CD players are the connections at the back of the drive and the buttons on the front.

You might be wondering how to get all the standard CD player options and buttons that are available on your hi-fi on your PC. These are actually provided by a program built into Windows XP called Windows Media Player.

You can listen to music while you work by playing a music CD in your computer. Other programs, such as Word or Excel, will run quite happily while a CD is playing.

This feature-packed program pops up automatically when a music CD is inserted and gives you all the functions of a conventional CD player, and more.

In addition to music CDs, the Windows Media Player also appears if you double-click on some other Multimedia files, including many video and recorded sound clips.

● Video show

One of the most visible differences when comparing your hi-fi to your PC is that Windows Media Player can provide an on-screen light show that accompanies the music. You can choose anything from multi-coloured kaleidoscopic patterns to cloudy whirlpools (see page 26).

(see page 26)

AUTOMATIC PLAY

The first time you insert an audio CD into your Windows XP computer, a dialog box may pop up asking what you want to do with the CD. To play the music, select the first option (Play Audio CD). Before clicking on the OK button, tick the Always do selected action option so that Windows doesn't ask this for every CD.

The visual effects go beyond the light show – you can completely alter the appearance of the Windows Media Player window itself. Whereas most windows appear on screen as rounded rectangle shapes, applying a skin completely transforms the player from an old-fashioned table-top radio into a weird and wacky floating head.

WHAT IT MEANS

SKIN

A skin is a computer file that modifies the appearance of a program. The program's features remain unchanged, but it can look completely different. Many skins are created by enthusiasts and are available for download from the Internet.

● Playing and recording

Whereas skins and visualizations are simply for fun, Windows Media Player has many capabilities that help to make listening to music on your PC a lot more convenient. For example, you can create hard disk versions of your favourite CD tracks so that you can play them at any time without having to insert the original music CD into the CD-ROM drive.

The big benefit is that a CD-ROM can store just over an hour of music, but an average hard disk can store dozens – even hundreds – of hours of music. Once you have recorded your music, the Windows Media Player can act as your own personal jukebox, allowing you to compile your own playlists from a mix of your favourite CDs. While it may also be possible to write your own CDs on your PC, be careful not to break any copyright rules.

Not all windows are square – this floating shape is the Windows Media Player reshaped with the Atomic skin.

Windows Media Player's main options

With capabilities that go far beyond simply playing music CDs, the Windows Media Player is designed to be the centre of your Multimedia entertainment.

● Now Playing
This is the main screen and shows the light show and a listing of the tracks.

● Media Guide
Connects you to a Web page that links you to many entertainment sources for movies, music files and other entertainment news.

● Copy from CD
Use this button to switch to the screen that lets you record tracks from the CD on to your hard disk.

● Media Library
All the media files on your PC can be viewed using this button. You can also create and save playlists of groups of tracks.

● Radio Tuner
Windows Media Player can also tune into music and speech transmitted through Internet radio broadcasts.

● Copy to CD or Device
This lets you create your own compilation CDs (if your PC has a CD writer) or copy tracks to a portable MP3 player.

● Skin Chooser
Click here to see the many wild and wonderful forms that Windows Media Player can assume.

Windows Media Player gives you an on-screen show to accompany the music of your choice.

SHORT CUTS

TV and CD player remote controls always have a mute button which enables you to silence the sound. Media Player is no different – press [F8] to toggle the mute on and off. In addition, pressing the [F9] key decreases the volume and [F10] increases it.

Playing music CDs

Insert an audio CD into your computer, and you can have music playing in the background while you work or sit back and watch a mesmerizing light show.

1 When you put a music CD in the CD-ROM drive, Windows Media Player automatically starts and the music begins to play. The central panel of the opening screen displays a pulsating light show that changes with the beat of the music.

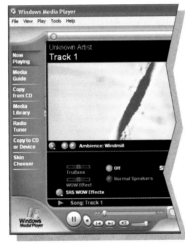

2 The Media Player comes with dozens of different light shows, called visualizations. Click on the Next visualization button in the middle of the window to work through them until you find one that suits your mood and music.

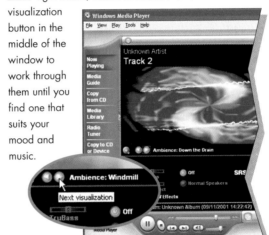

PC TIPS

If you just want to listen to background music while you work, the light show is likely to be very distracting. Click on the Minimize button on the Windows Media Player Title bar to shrink the window down to a button on the Taskbar. The music will carry on playing.

3 The Play/Pause, Stop, Next and Previous buttons work just like the controls on a hi-fi's CD player. Click on them to control the play back of the tracks on your CD.

4 You can also choose tracks using the track listing on the right of the window. For example, double-click on a track and it starts to play immediately. If you right-click on it, a pop-up menu gives other options – such as changing the playing order with the Move Up and Move Down commands.

5 If you'd like to change the whole appearance of the Windows Media Player, you can do that too. Click on the Switch to skin mode button near the bottom of the window and the player takes on a funkier, less window-like, shape. All of the most important controls are still available.

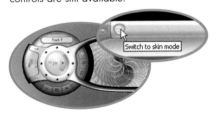

6 Windows XP comes with a number of skins. To change the Media Player's skin, you should first double-click on the button at the bottom right of the Desktop to revert to Windows Media Player's normal window. Then click on the Skin Chooser button on the left of this window to see the options available.

7 Click on one of the skins that is now listed in the middle of the window. A panel on the right gives you a preview (see inset below). When you find one you like, double-click on it to use it.

FULL SCREEN LIGHT SHOW

To make the most of the Windows Media Player visualizations, click on the View full screen button just to the left of the track list. The Desktop disappears and you can see the full effect of the visualization. Press the [Esc] key to switch back to the normal view.

Copying CD tracks to your hard disk

Most modern computers have plenty of hard disk space so you can store music here to avoid having to insert a CD when you want to play your favourite tracks.

1 Put a music CD into your CD-ROM drive and when the Windows Media Player starts, click on the Copy from CD button on the left of the window. Your computer prompts you to connect to the Internet. This is because it can download information about the CD from an online database.

2 Within a few moments of being connected, a panel appears under the track listing. The online database covers most popular CDs. Click on the Finish button and Windows Media Player will download the necessary information from the database.

COPYRIGHT AND PIRACY

The idea behind ripping tracks from CD to your hard disk is convenience; being able to listen to music from several albums without having to swap CDs. It is not designed for piracy – the illegal copying of copyrighted music. You are not supposed to copy your favourite tracks and then sell or swap the original CD.

3 The track listing now shows the names of the songs and other information, such as the songwriter and music genre. You can now disconnect from the Internet.

4 Initially, the program assumes you want to copy all of the tracks to your hard disk. Remove the ticks next to those tracks you don't want. If you need to remind yourself which track is which, just double-click to hear it. When you've made your selections, click on the Copy Music button to **rip** the tracks.

5 The Copy Status column shows progress. You won't hear the track as it's being recorded because the ripping process happens very quickly.

6 Remove this CD and repeat the process for your other favourite tracks. When you've finished, click on the Media Library button on the left of the window. Click on the All Audio icon in the centre panel to see all the music tracks on your computer's hard disk.

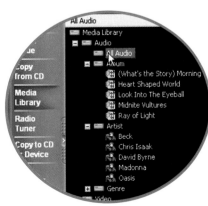

7 Double-click on any track to listen to it. Click on the Now Playing screen to see the visualization along with all the tracks you have ripped.

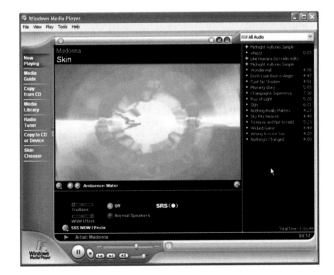

WHAT IT MEANS

RIP

This means to copy the digital data on an audio CD on to your computer's hard disk. When Windows Media Player rips a CD, it copies it in a format known as Windows Media Audio and compresses it to save space.

Software

Microsoft® Word

Microsoft® Excel

CorelDRAW ®

Customizing your toolbars

Microsoft Word usually displays two toolbars, but it can show more. You can even create your own customized toolbar to help you use the program more effectively.

The beauty of using a mouse with Windows programs is that you don't need to scroll through a long list of menu options to look for a tool or command. Almost all programs have a row of one-click buttons that enable you to access the most commonly used commands. These useful buttons are combined into toolbars.

Word is no different: it has two toolbars beneath the menu bar. These are the Standard and Formatting toolbars; on some versions of Word you'll find them on one line, on others they may be one on top of the other. They allow you to select many of Word's commands with just a single click of the mouse button. Many of the buttons on the Standard and Formatting toolbars are similar to those in Excel, CorelDRAW and other Windows programs.

For example, the buttons on the Standard toolbar include basic commands, such as Open, Save, Print, Cut, Paste and Help. These commands are not directly related to changing the appearance or formatting of the text in your documents manually. For that, you use the buttons on the Formatting toolbar, where you'll find commands such as Bold, Italics and Underline.

● **Other tools**
There are also other toolbars available within Word that you might not find in other programs. Some will appear on your screen automatically; others, such as the Drawing toolbar, can be called up simply by clicking on the Drawing button on the Standard toolbar.

You can also use the Toolbar command on the View menu to open toolbars. When you use this command, the toolbars will remain visible until you

Using the Drawing tools in Word you can create shapes, change them and fill them with colour. Click on the Drawing button to bring up the toolbar.

WHAT IT MEANS

SUBSCRIPT AND
SUPERSCRIPT

*Subscript and
superscript are the
terms used to describe
text characters that sit
below or above the line
on which normal text
sits. The trademark
symbol (as in
CorelDRAW₍TM₎) is a
subscript character.*

switch them off. This can be useful if you're frequently changing from one activity to another and don't like the toolbars appearing and disappearing. We show Word's extra toolbars below. You will find some with buttons that help you to jazz up your documents and some that are more suitable for business users as they include buttons for producing forms and working with database information. You'll soon find which of the functions are the most useful for you.

● **Make your own toolbars**
Word also allows you to create custom toolbars. This is particularly useful if you find you use a variety of buttons from a number of different toolbars. By combining your favourite buttons into one personalized toolbar, you can work much more quickly and efficiently. We show you how to create your own toolbar on page 33.

If you don't want to create a whole new toolbar from scratch, you can just add extra buttons to Word's existing toolbars. For example, if you often use the subscript and superscript options, it helps to have these available on an accessible toolbar.

If your toolbars are currently on two lines, a useful way to gain more screen space is to place them on one line (see Space saver box, page 32). Alternatively, make your own custom toolbar and hide any buttons you don't need.

Introducing Word's other toolbars

Drawing
The Drawing toolbar allows you to draw simple diagrams and pictures using Word's drawing tools. You can also choose from a range of pre-set shapes, which you can then adjust and colour however you want.

Tables and Borders
This toolbar lets you format and create simple tables with borders around them. You can even put borders or frames around individual words in the text if you want.

Picture
This toolbar allows you to brighten up your letters, essays and other documents by inserting graphics. Pictures can be imported into Word from other programs, such as Paint or CorelDRAW, and then adjusted in size once they are in place on the page.

WordArt
The WordArt toolbar provides lots of options for creating special text effects. These are great for producing banners or greetings cards or anything where you want the text to really stand out.

More advanced toolbars

There are special toolbars that can help you to create more complex documents.

Reviewing
This feature allows you to track changes made to your document and to undo them. It also lets you add comments and highlights that can't be seen by other readers.

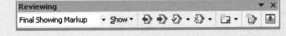

Web
The most recent versions of Word were created with the Internet in mind. You can easily insert links in your documents to the World Wide Web using this toolbar, and even access your Web browser options.

Database
The Database toolbar is for inserting and altering complex tables. It is of more use to business rather than home users.

Visual Basic
Visual Basic is a simple programming language for use in conjunction with Word. Unless you're a programmer, you're unlikely to find these commands useful.

Control toolbox
This toolbar allows you to insert objects, such as check boxes and radio buttons, into your document, which can be particularly useful when creating forms or linked files, for instance.

Forms
This toolbar is similar to the Control toolbox, except that it is dedicated to creating a variety of forms. If your document has a form in it, the information can be transferred to other programs, such as Microsoft Excel.

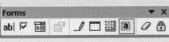

Arranging the toolbars

You don't have to accept the on-screen arrangement of toolbars that comes with Word. It's easy to put the tools you want where you want.

THE STANDARD and Formatting toolbars that Word displays by default can be moved anywhere on the screen. If you move a toolbar to one of the screen's other edges, it will lock against that edge. When a toolbar is not positioned at an edge, it is said to be floating. You can re-shape a floating toolbar so that it occupies a more convenient area on screen.

1 Let's bring up one of the hidden toolbars on screen. From the View menu, select Toolbars and choose the AutoText toolbar (AutoText is a system of customization that allows you to enter frequently used text or pictures at the click of a button). The new toolbar (right) will appear, floating on your screen.

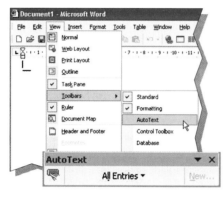

SPACE SAVER

In a new installation of XP, Word will place the Standard and Formatting toolbars on the same row. If, however, in a previous version of Word you had the toolbars on two rows, this setting may remain; to save space, you can place them on the same row.

Go to the View menu and select Customize at the bottom of the Toolbars sub-menu. Then, in the Customize dialog box, click on the tick by the Show Standard and Formatting toolbars on two rows option to cancel the command.

2 You can move a toolbar around by clicking on the dark beige bar and holding down the left mouse button; if you now move the mouse, the toolbar will also move. Release the mouse button when you have moved it to its new location.

3 If you want to change the shape of a floating toolbar, move your cursor to the edge of the toolbar until it changes into a double-headed arrow. Keep your finger on the left mouse button, move the cursor up and down, and the toolbar changes shape.

PC TIPS

Toolbars for your templates

In Stage 1, pages 38–41, we showed you how to create templates to use as the basis for similar documents. You can also add different toolbar set-ups to different templates. You could then have, for example, a template for invoices, with lots of formatting buttons; or a template for shopping lists with lots of tables buttons, and so on. Just arrange the toolbar to your liking and save the template as you usually do.

4 You can close a toolbar by clicking on the standard 'X' button in the top right-hand corner. You get the toolbar back by using the View menu again (see Step 1).

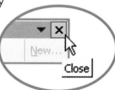

5 To move an existing toolbar, click on the vertical shaded bar at the far left of the toolbar and keep your mouse button pressed down while you move it.

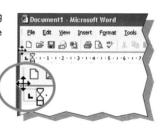

6 Move the mouse down and to the right and you will find that the toolbar moves with the mouse. Release the mouse button and the toolbar will appear as a floating toolbar, just like the AutoText toolbar in Steps 1 and 2.

7 To lock a toolbar back in place, move it to one of the edges of the Word window; when you release the mouse button, the bar will lock in place, either vertically or horizontally.

8 You can even put two toolbars on the same line. Just move a floating toolbar to the right of an existing toolbar. (You should only do this if there seems to be enough space for the extra buttons.)

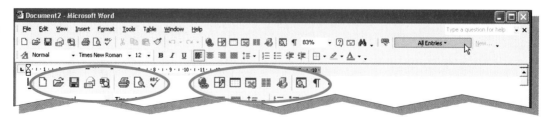

How to customize the toolbars

As well as controlling which toolbars are displayed on screen, you can also create your own customized toolbar containing your choice of buttons.

1 Here we remove the Insert Microsoft Excel Worksheet button (which is next to the Insert Table button). Hold down the [Alt] key, click on the button on the toolbar and drag it away from the bar. When you let go of the mouse, the button will have been removed from the toolbar.

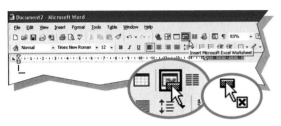

2 To add new commands to a toolbar, go to the View menu, select Toolbars and then choose Customize (at the bottom of the second drop-down menu).

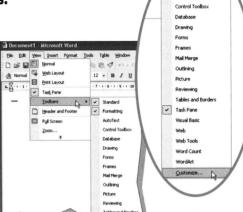

3 Select the Toolbars tab at the top of the window. Make sure that the Standard toolbar is ticked in the Toolbars list and then select the Commands tab.

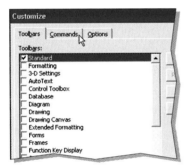

4 We are going to add a **Save All** button. Click on File in the Categories list, and scroll down the Commands list until you find the Save All command.

WHAT IT MEANS

SAVE ALL
This command saves changes to all the Word documents that are currently open. The normal Save command saves the changes only in the document that you are working on.

5 Click on the Save All button and drag it on to the toolbar. A vertical black bar will appear as you drag the button to show you where the button will appear when you drop it.

6 To move buttons from one toolbar to another, use the [Alt] key as shown in Step 1, but drag the button to a new position on another toolbar instead.

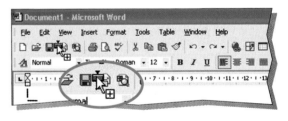

7 As you move more and more buttons to a single toolbar, you might find it convenient to delete a whole toolbar. This can free space and let you see more of your document. Go to the View menu, select the Toolbars option and then Customize. Click on the Toolbars tab, select the toolbar you want to delete and click on the Delete button. You'll find this can be done only with custom toolbars; the default toolbars can be altered, but they cannot be deleted altogether.

8 To hide one of the default toolbars so that it no longer appears on your Word screen, turn it into a floating toolbar by dragging it from the top of the screen into the main area of the Word screen (as in Step 6 on page 32), then simply click on the close button at the top right of the toolbar.

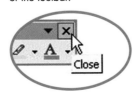

PC TIPS

Default settings

If you find you've deleted buttons and toolbars you need, you can reset things to the way they were when you first installed Word. Simply go to the View menu, click on Toolbars, then Customize and ensure that the Toolbars tab is selected. From there, click on the toolbar you want to reset, click on the Reset button and all the toolbar settings you have changed will be reset to their original state.

Microsoft® Word

Customizing your menus

We have already seen how to customize Word's toolbars (see pages 30–33). By adding and removing buttons from the standard toolbars, as well as creating brand new toolbars, we have shown you how to alter Word's toolbar options to suit the way you work. Exactly the same thing can also be done with the drop-down menus and their options.

This means that, depending on which settings you choose, you can alter your own copy of Word so much that it can become almost unrecognizable to other users, while at the same time working to your exact specifications and preferences.

● Adding to a menu

There are nine built-in, drop-down menus displayed on the menu bar. Although their contents might seem fixed, these menus can all be altered just as easily as altering toolbars, and by using the same tools. The Customize window, with its list of Categories and Commands, makes adding a new command to a menu a simple case of dragging and dropping the command. Moving a command from menu to menu or deleting one entirely is just as easy to achieve.

● Changing and moving menus

The same principles can be applied to a whole menu, allowing you to delete it or move it wherever you want. You can add any of the pre-set menus to the menu bar. You can even create multiple versions of the same menu that offer different options.

It is also possible to create custom menus that house their own commands. This is useful if you want to keep your most commonly used functions in one menu or if you want to create a new set of commands.

In our exercise opposite, we show how to add a line spacing command to the Format menu. This is an operation that usually takes a number of separate mouse clicks to activate, so if you use it regularly you can save a lot of time. We also show how to add this command to the menu bar, where it will be available with a click or two of the mouse. The same principle applies to other commands – so with only a little tinkering, you can quickly create your own made-to-measure menus.

Word offers you plenty of ways to customize its settings so that it works in the way you prefer. Here we show you how to alter the menu options to suit your needs.

Adding a menu option

In this example, we show how to add a useful command to the Format menu and how to create a whole new menu. The same principles apply to adding other options.

1 We are going to customize the Format menu by adding an option for 1.5 line spacing (you could just as easily add double line spacing if you prefer). Ordinarily, this function can be accessed only by going through a number of sub-menus, but we'll put the option directly on the Format menu. Start by clicking on Customize in the Tools menu.

2 When the Customize dialog box appears, click on the Commands tab. This gives a list of Categories on the left and Commands on the right. Line spacing is in the Format category, so click on that and scroll down the commands list to find 1.5 Spacing.

PC TIPS

You can change menus as much and as often as you like because you can always return to the original menus.

Go to the Built-in Menus option, near the bottom of the Categories list. This shows you all the standard menus and you can then drag and drop your choice onto the toolbar and use it to replace your customized version.

Microsoft® Word

3 Drag the 1.5 Spacing command over the Format menu button and the full menu will drop down. If you keep your finger on the mouse button you'll find that a black horizontal line appears in the menu options. This indicates where the new menu option will appear when you let go of the mouse. Place the 1.5 Spacing command on the Format menu by letting go of the mouse button. When you've finished, you can close the Customize dialog box.

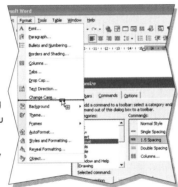

4 Type some text into a blank document, highlight it and then go to the Format menu. You will now see your new menu option. Select it and your text will reflect the new format.

5 To move an existing menu command, open the Customize dialog box and find the menu command (see Step 2). Then drag and drop it to a different position on the menu or to a different menu entirely. To delete a command, drag and drop it from the menu on to the main Word document.

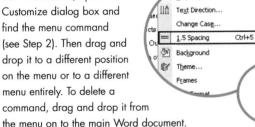

6 A whole menu can be deleted just by dragging and dropping the menu's name from the toolbar onto the main Word document. Here we are deleting the Format menu.

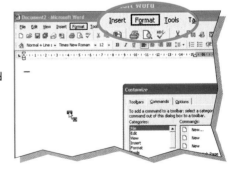

7 If you want to create a completely new menu, go right to the end of the Categories list in the Customize dialog box and select the New Menu entry. Drag it onto the toolbar next to an existing menu.

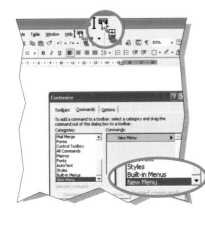

8 The new menu is simply called New Menu. To change it to something more meaningful, click on it with the right mouse button. A list of options appears and you can type a suitable word into the Name text box.

9 Now you can use exactly the same procedure we showed in Steps 2–3 to add commands to your new menu.

Seeing more in Word

If you'd like to clear your screen of clutter and make more space for your documents, why not make use of Word's Full Screen option?

If your computer has a 14- or 15-inch monitor, you might find that there's not always a lot of space to display your document. This is especially true if you are working with a screen resolution of 640x480. With a complex program such as Word, a great deal of the screen is taken up with toolbars, buttons and scrollbars, leaving a much smaller area for typing. For example, with a 640x480 resolution screen and a 14-inch monitor, Word provides a 12x27cm area for typing, out of a possible 20x28cm. This is just 42 per cent of the total screen area.

● Removing toolbars
If you want to see more of your letters and documents, there are several ways to get a larger area to work in. The Windows Taskbar is normally set to appear on top of whichever program you are using, but you can switch this off very easily (see Stage 2, pages 14–17). This gives you a little more room at the bottom of the screen.

You can also try switching off the toolbars to stop them from appearing on the screen (see pages 30–33). This isn't a perfect option – you lose access to many useful buttons – but you will be able to see just how much of the typing area you lose to them (below). A much better idea is to use Word's Full Screen mode. This provides you with a blank screen to type on.

Select the Full Screen option from the View menu. To return to the normal view, press the [Esc] key, or click on the Close Full Screen button on the tiny floating toolbar (the only distraction that appears on screen).

● Switching your views
You can switch views, depending on the type of work you are doing, for example, using full screen views when typing and switching to normal mode to add styling and formatting with the toolbars and menus. Full Screen mode

Your screen doesn't have to be cluttered with icons and tools. There are various ways of getting rid of them to leave you a clean, uncluttered space in which to work.

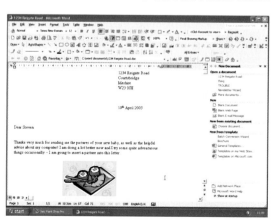

The Word screen (near left) has more toolbars than usual on display and, when compared with the other screen (far left), it shows clearly how much screen space is lost if you keep too many toolbars on your screen.

Microsoft® Word

gives you a lot of extra space but, without menus or toolbars, you'll need to find other ways to access Word's editing and formatting options (see Shortcuts, right). There are two methods: the first is to click the right mouse button and Word will produce a menu of frequently used commands for you to choose from.

Alternatively, you can view the menus only when you need them. When you move your pointer to the top of the screen, the menu bar will appear. Select the command you want and then the menu bar will disappear, restoring your full screen view.

S H O R T C U T S

Keyboard shortcuts are especially useful when you're in Full Screen mode. You get quick access to common commands without having to move your mouse at all. It doesn't matter that you can't see the menus – the commands will still work perfectly. Here are some very useful shortcuts.

[Ctrl]+[N]	New	[Ctrl]+[C]	Copy
[Ctrl]+[O]	Open	[Ctrl]+[X]	Cut
[Ctrl]+[S]	Save	[Ctrl]+[V]	Paste
[Ctrl]+[P]	Print	[Ctrl]+[B]	Bold
[Ctrl]+[Z]	Undo	[Ctrl]+[I]	Italics
[Ctrl]+[A]	Select all	[Ctrl]+[U]	Underline

PC TIPS

Full Screen Button

If you find you use Full Screen mode a lot, you might want to add it as a button to one of the toolbars. On pages 30–33, we described how to customize Word's toolbars. Here's how to add the Full Screen Mode button: from the View menu, select Toolbars and choose the Customize option. From the dialog box that now appears, choose the Commands tab and select the View category. The list on the right shows the commands that are in the View menu. Scroll down this list to the Full Screen button and drag it onto one of the toolbars (see below).

Using Word's Full Screen view

Seeing more of your document on the screen can help you prepare your work more quickly and clearly – it's easy to get a full screen view of your work in progress.

1 Here's a Word document as it normally appears. As you can see, space for several lines of text is taken up by the working parts of the Word window, such as the title bar, menu bar, two toolbars and status line. All of these considerably reduce the space you have for working on your document.

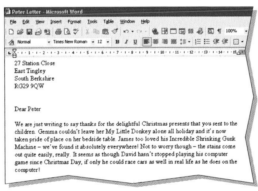

2 To see the difference that Full Screen mode can make, go to the View menu and select the Full Screen command.

3 Your document will now take up the whole of the screen. All of the screen clutter has disappeared, leaving just one small floating toolbar. This view will help you to concentrate on the document itself. We can now see a lot more of our letter on screen.

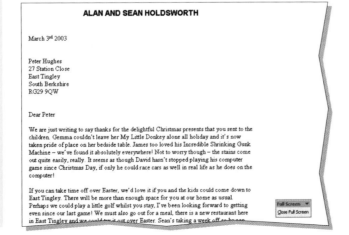

4 Move the mouse pointer to the top of the screen and you will see Word's menu bar automatically reappear (below). Choose your

commands and the menu bar will automatically disappear again. To switch back out of Full Screen mode, click on the Close Full Screen option on the floating toolbar that remains on your screen. Pressing [Esc] on your keyboard also moves you back to the normal viewing mode.

Using fields in Word

Fields are powerful, flexible tools that enable you to set up coded instructions so Word can carry out a variety of operations automatically.

Dear Jack and Sarah

We've already seen how useful fields can be when setting up a mail merge (see Stage 3, pages 50–53). In that example, we put several fields in a document as place markers in order to tell Word where we wanted name and address details inserted. However, there are many other ways to use fields.

● **Field uses**

In very simple terms, fields are just coded instructions that Word can recognize, act upon and then replace with the appropriate text or numbers. The big advantage is that once you have set up a field, you can use it to import information any time you want to work on the document, thus updating it automatically. At the simplest and most common level, you can add fields which update data that is readily available on your computer: for example, inserting today's date or automatically updating page numbers.

HIDDEN FIELDS

Apart from mail merging, you will be surprised at just how often you have used fields already – probably without even knowing it. For example, more than half of the items on the Insert menu are field-related, even though the relevant dialog boxes don't mention the fact and the codes are normally hidden from view.

If you wish, you can ask Word to show you any field codes on the page (see page 40). The fields are very easy to spot as they are enclosed on either side by curly brackets – { thus } – which are known as braces (right). However, you can't just type a field code on to a page. You must apply it in the correct way from the relevant dialog box.

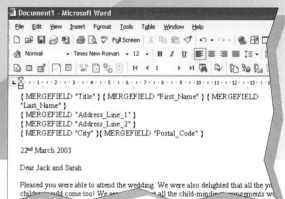

● **Advanced calculations**

At a more complex level, fields can be used to co-ordinate multiple documents or documents with multiple parts. Mail merge is an obvious example of this, as name and address fields are used to call up the relevant details from a separate data document and produce personalized letters for a bulk mailing.

Even more advanced fields are used when you create indexes, tables of contents, footnotes and figure references, for example, in long or complex documents. However, the basic principle is that Word lets you mark any relevant text or figures in the document. It is then able to tabulate or index the entries automatically.

You can cross-reference documents in a similar way, perhaps creating a field that refers the reader to another part of the document. You can even add a link that takes the reader there with a single click.

Word also has some more advanced fields that look similar to the functions used in Microsoft Excel. In fact, Word is able to use fields to work out quite complex formulae that employ other, sometimes variable, factors also enclosed in fields. For example, using fields you can create a table of sales figures that adds itself up. The table could even work out gross sales and profits and then insert the results in specific places that you have marked elsewhere in the document.

● **See what's possible**

Most of the examples above are quite involved applications for a word processor because they embrace spreadsheet formula components, such as functions and operators, as well as tables, bookmarks and so on. Have a look at the Field dialog box (below) to get an idea of the diverse ways in which fields can be used.

The more complex uses for fields will be covered later in the course, but over the next two pages we will deal with a couple of the more basic and widely applicable ones.

The Field dialog box

To get an idea of how powerful and complex fields can be, call up the Field dialog box from Word's Insert menu. Click on each category in turn and you will see a description of the function at the bottom of the dialog box.

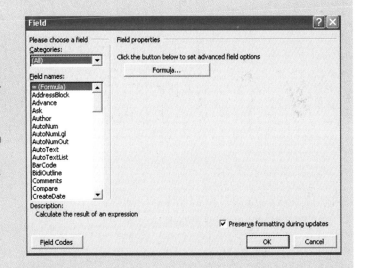

Date and Time

This inserts the date and/or time the document was created, the current date or time, the total editing time and the date the document was last printed or saved. Customize the date/time display by choosing a format in the Field Properties list on the right of the dialog box.

Document Automation

This is a complex collection of functions. Compare allows you to assess the results of other fields – for example, you could set it to trawl through a list of customers and find those with a credit rating above a set amount. The other functions are much more advanced and are mainly for business users.

Document Information

This calls in information specified elsewhere in Word, such as the number of words in the current document.

Equations and Formulas

This inserts spreadsheet-style formulae.

Index and Tables

These are used to create an index or list of contents for one or more documents, and also to mark the relevant entries. These features can be very useful and save time.

Links and References

This allows you to insert bookmarked text, a hyperlink or a picture into any Word document.

Mail Merge

An advanced feature for documents that you can use for sending letters to a number of people, without having to amend each letter individually (see Stage 3, pages 50–53).

Numbering

This lets you number paragraphs and sections as well as enter additional numerical information, such as how many times a document has been saved.

User Information

This lets you insert information that comes from the Options dialog box. For example, if you have already typed your address details into Word's Options dialog box, you can insert them as a field instead of retyping them every time you need them (see page 41).

Adding time, date and page fields

Here we'll see how to set up a document that automatically inserts the date and time and correctly numbers the pages.

1 Open a new document in Word. Click on the Insert menu and select Date and Time. The dialog box that pops up contains settings for various time and date formats. These show how the information will appear in your document. Click on the style that you want to use, tick the Update automatically box and then click on the OK button.

2 This puts a field in the document, displaying the date and time that you entered it. Save the page, close it, and open it again (here we have left it for several hours). Click on the field to select it and press the [F9] key to update the time and date information automatically.

3 Now select Options from the Tools menu. Click on the View tab and put a tick in the Field codes box. Click on the OK button to return to your document. You can now see the field that is generating the updated time/date stamp. However, whenever you print out the page, you'll see that it will always print the date and time, not the field code. Now hide the codes by repeating the procedure and unticking the Field codes box before you click on OK.

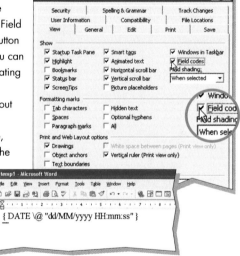

4 Go to the Insert menu again. Now select Page Numbers. Ensure that the Position box is set to Bottom of page (Footer) and that the Show number on first page option is checked. The Alignment box should show Right, to position the number to the right of the page. Then click on the OK button.

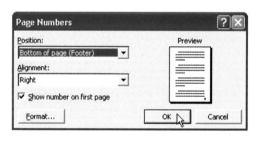

5 You will see that you now have a small page number at the bottom right of the page. You'll notice that it's grey and that you can't select it with the mouse pointer (as you can with other text in your document). That's because it's in a special part of the page, called a footer (see opposite).

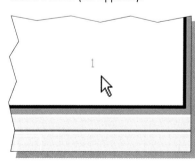

6 Now let's create a new page to see how it numbers automatically. Go to the Insert menu and select the Break command. In the dialog box that appears (below left) the Page break option is selected by default, so click on OK. When you return to your document, scroll down to the bottom of the new page and you'll see that the number 2 has automatically been inserted.

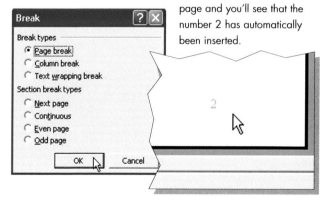

PC TIPS

Once you have created a field, you can treat it as if you had typed in the data yourself. This means you can cut and paste it, delete part of it or do anything you would do to normal text.

Entering user information

Here we create a letter that customizes itself, taking the User Information on the PC and inserting the name and address at the top.

WHAT IT MEANS

HEADER AND FOOTER

Headers and footers are special areas at the top and bottom of the page. They can be edited from the View menu. They are usually used in longer documents for inserting running headings at the top of the page, or page numbers at the bottom.

1 Create a new page and, from the Tools menu, select Options and click the User Information tab. This may already be filled in, but if it isn't, add your name, initials and address information; then click on the OK button at the bottom of the screen.

2 Now select Field from the Insert menu. In the dialog box that appears, look under Categories and select User Information. Under Field names, select UserAddress. Click on OK. The field will retrieve the address from your User Information and place it on the page.

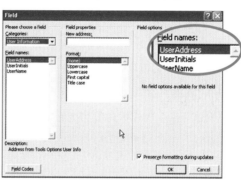

3 You can use the [Tab] key to move each line of the address over to the right. Underneath, place a suitable Date and Time field, as you did on page 40. Type in, or copy and paste, enough text to resemble a letter and then add a few blank lines at the bottom.

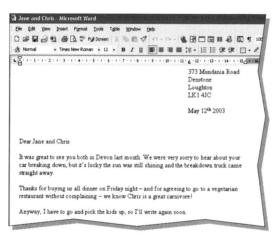

4 Call up the Field dialog box and select User Information again. This time choose UserName under Field names and click on OK. The field will then automatically retrieve the name from your User Information and place it on the page.

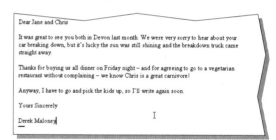

5 Now let's add a number to the bottom of the page. This time, we'll make it tell the reader whether to expect any more pages – this is very useful when faxing letters. Go to the View menu and select **Header and Footer**. A toolbar pops up and a header appears in the document. Click on the Switch between Header and Footer button on the toolbar to create a footer. Then click on the Insert AutoText button and select Page X of Y. Click on Close.

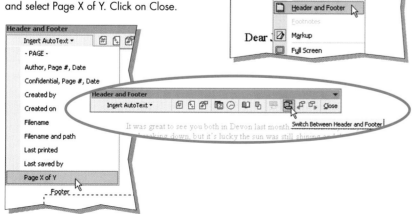

6 At the bottom of the page you will now see Page 1 of 1. If you add another page the first page will then say Page 1 of 2, and the second, Page 2 of 2. Word will update this automatically as you add more pages. If you want to apply a different font style to this text, double-click on it and you will then be able to select the text and the Header and Footer toolbar will appear again. Once you have accessed the footer, you can highlight and format this text as usual.

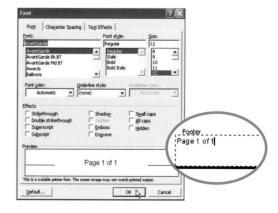

Saving files as Web pages

You can choose to save any of your documents as Web pages ready to place on your site, or create new Web pages from ready-made templates.

Internet service providers almost always include some free Web space as part of the service, so why not make use of it? If you want to create Web pages, you don't need any special software – Word includes all the features you'll need to get started. Creating a Web page is no harder than creating any other type of document (see Stage 3, pages 132–135). You can convert any existing Word document to a Web page, or create Web pages from scratch using Word's Web Page Wizard.

Whichever you choose, Word adds all the necessary HTML (short for HyperText Markup Language) codes to the text and images. You don't need to know any of the technical aspects of HTML, so even a Net novice can quickly achieve impressive results.

WEB EDITORS

Although many people – even professionals – use a word processor to create pages for the Internet, there are dozens of specialized Web editors. Many are shareware (free programs, at least for a time), while others are add-ons for PCs or desktop-publishing programs.

Most Web editors include a text editor with automated functions for adding components, such as pictures and hyperlinks, plus a viewer to see the finished product. This is essential because it shows how a page will appear in the browser. Examples include CoffeeCup's HTML editor and Sausage Software's HotDog, both of which are shareware. However, an increasing number of editors employ what is known as WYSIWYG (see What it Means box, right) which allows you to create a Web page and see the results instantly – without the need for a viewer. Word, to some extent, is a WYSIWYG Web editor.

● How Word uses codes

At the simplest level, HTML codes specify that a section of text exists in, say, bold or italic. At its most complex, the code can create a page that is full of pictures and tables.

Word already uses its own, similar codes in much the same way. When you format an ordinary document, Word assigns codes to the file. It hides these codes from you but your keyboard commands add and remove them.

Word XP includes the Save as Web Page menu command for saving documents in HTML format. This converts the document into the required format, and lets you add HTML-specific information (see opposite).

● Complex layouts

The Save as Web Page command works best for simple Web pages. The reason is that, while Word allows you to create complex designs with overlapping text boxes and picture frames, HTML lacks many of the advanced layout features and may not be able to properly represent complicated Word layouts. For advanced Web page design, a dedicated Web editor is best (see box, left).

WHAT IT MEANS

WYSIWYG

WYSIWYG stands for What You See Is What You Get – in other words, what you see on screen looks exactly the same as the output version. Traditionally, this would have meant the version printed on paper but today the final output could just as easily be a Web site.

Experimenting with HTML pages

Here we see how to create a simple document, save it in Web page format and view the result. We also explore some limitations of HTML.

IF YOU have prepared a document that you would like to be included in a Web site, the simplest way to see if it works is to save it as an HTML file and view it using your Web browser software (such as Netscape Navigator or Microsoft Internet Explorer). The result is often perfectly acceptable, although it can look slightly different from the document you would get if you printed out the page. Here we look at what kind of results you can expect.

1 Let's suppose that you have created a simple document with some images and formatted text. For our example, we've just inserted a piece of clip art, added a headline and then formatted a short list of contents modelled on a newsletter. It doesn't matter how complex your page is for the purposes of this exercise.

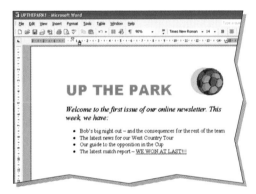

2 Select Save as Web Page from the File menu. When the Save As dialog box appears, choose a folder for your Web page – we've opted for a misc documents folder (below). Type a suitable name into the File name box, but before clicking on the Save button, click on the Change Title button.

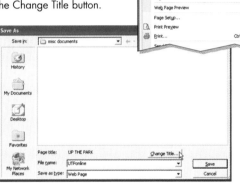

3 Use the Set Page Title dialog box to add the text you want to appear in the Title bar of the Web browser when people look at your Web page. Click on the OK button and then on the Save button in the Save As dialog box to return to your Web page.

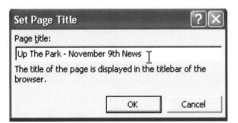

4 To see what your Web page will look like when viewed on the Internet, select Web Page Preview from the File menu.

5 Word launches Internet Explorer and your Web page loads automatically. With simple layouts like this one, the page appears almost exactly the same as the document you started with originally (see Step 1).

Bullet point lists

Word's bullet points are a simple and effective way of giving clarity and an extra professional punch to ideas and lists. Here's how to use them.

A bullet point is simply a small shape – typically a dot like this ● – that you use to highlight items in a list. With a bullet indicating the beginning of each item, you can see at a glance how many points there are in the list and where each begins.

Bullets stand out much more clearly than standard keyboard characters, such as dashes, and look much more elegant than underlining. Bullet points are emphatic and help ensure that an important list doesn't get lost in a long letter or document. It is no coincidence that bullet point lists are frequently used in all types of important business documents. You can also use them to give extra punch and emphasis when listing important points in many and various kinds of home documents, from key points in school essays to a list of tasks for someone looking after your house while you're on holiday.

● Bullet styles
Bullets usually take the form of large black dots, but you can choose from a whole range

of different sizes, shapes and colours (ours, for example, are stars in circles). If you want to make your letters and documents look truly unique, you can even make your very own style of bullet points. Word also enables you to insert numbered lines instead of bullet points. The numbering option is especially useful if you want to refer back to these points later on in the document.

Although you can add bullets as you go through (see Automatic bullets box, left), they are easy to add to a list you have already created. In most cases, you need only press a single button. Even with numbering, one command can number the entire list. Word will then automatically move on to the next number every time you press the [Enter] key to add a new item. Even if you add a new item in the middle of the list, Word will automatically renumber the rest of the list.

AUTOMATIC BULLETS

Word allows you to add bullet points to a list as you type it in. To do this, start a new line by typing an asterisk (*), a space and then the words for the first item in your list. As soon as you press the [Enter] key to start a new point, the asterisk will turn into a bullet.

Type the next item in your list and it will also be bulleted – you don't need to type the asterisk or the space. To stop the automatic bulleting – so you can start typing normal paragraphs of text – press the [Delete] key at the start of a new line.

Making a bullet point list

In this step-by-step example, we show you how to add various styles of bullet to a list of tasks for someone who's looking after the house while you're away on holiday.

1 First type in a sample document. We have created a letter that includes a list of pointers. There's also a short introduction to the letter, which doesn't need bullets.

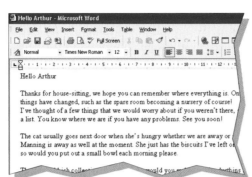

2 To add the bullets, first select the text of your list. Do this by moving your mouse pointer to the left of the first line and clicking and holding down the left button. Then move the cursor over the whole list until all the text is highlighted.

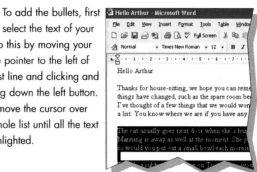

3 Click on the Bullets button on the Formatting toolbar. A standard bullet appears at the start of each paragraph and the text moves over to fit it in.

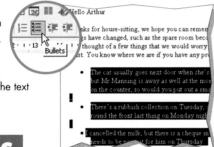

4 You can easily change the appearance of these bullet points. Click on the Format menu and then select the Bullets and Numbering command from the drop-down list.

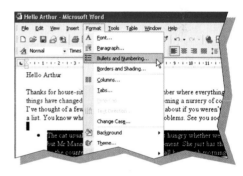

PC TIPS

Removing bullets from a list is as easy as adding them. First, select the bulleted text (as shown in Step 2), then click on the Bullets button on the toolbar once more. The bullets will disappear from the list of items and your text will look normal once again.

5 Click on the picture of the particular style of bullet you want to use and then on the Customize button.

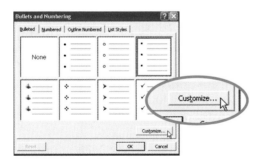

6 The Customize Bulleted List dialog box pops up. Click on the Font button on the left, under Bullet character.

7 You can choose any character from any of the typefaces on your PC. Here, we've selected Wingdings. Once you've chosen, click on OK.

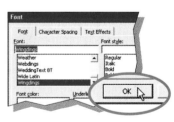

8 Click on the Character button to see the huge range of symbols in Wingdings. Click on any of the shapes that takes your fancy – we've chosen a circle with a star in it. Then click on OK to make that shape into your standard bullet point.

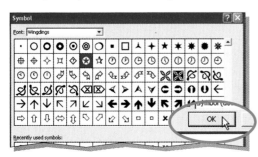

9 Before returning to your letter, you can also adjust the amount of space between the side of the page and the bullets using the two small arrow buttons next to the Indent at: box under Bullet position. To adjust the space between the bullets and the text, use the arrows by the Text position boxes.

10 Click on the OK button on each dialog box that's open. Once they're all closed, you'll see your custom bullet points in place in the text.

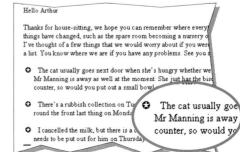

Introducing Excel functions

In order to benefit from Excel's full potential, it's worth getting to know about some of its more powerful tools.

W e've already seen how to carry out mathematical calculations using some of the formulae contained within Excel (see Stage 1, pages 54–55). Most of these examples involved using the basic arithmetic symbols for addition (+), subtraction (-), multiplication (∗) and division (/).

However, Excel also includes a range of more powerful operators, which make it possible to carry out even more useful and complicated formulae. These operators are known as functions.

In fact, we've already encountered some examples of Excel functions. For instance, we saw how to add up a column of figures by using the AutoSum button in the Standard Toolbar (see Stage 1, pages 62–63). As its name suggests, the AutoSum function automates the process of adding up a list of figures. To do so, it uses a function called SUM. If you look at a cell where you've used AutoSum, you will find that it contains a formula that looks something like =SUM(B2:B5).

● **How functions work**
Like most other functions, SUM cannot produce a result without being given further instructions. The information it needs is contained in a pair of brackets that follow the name of the function (cell references B2:B5 as shown, right). Each information item used by a function is called an argument and can be a cell reference, a number or even text.

As this suggests, functions deal with much more than just arithmetic. For example, there is a function called PMT, which works out loan repayments, and a function called MONTH to convert a number from 1 to 12 into a month. Excel organizes its functions into nine groups: Financial; Date & Time; Math & Trig; Statistical; Lookup & Reference; Database; Text; Logical; and Information. Each group contains a number of functions related to that topic. For example, PMT is in the Financial group and MONTH can be found under Date & Time.

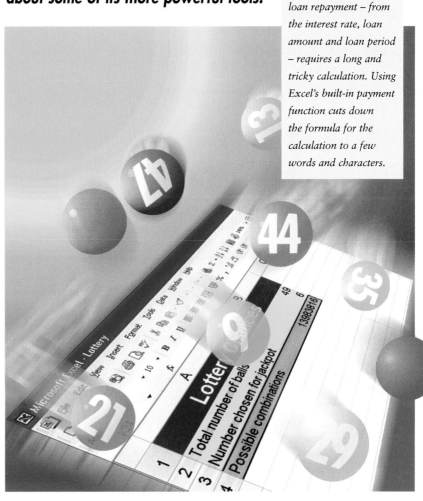

● **Using functions**
You can include any function in the formulae you create in the Formula Bar. All you have to do is click on the Insert Function button in the Standard Toolbar (it looks like a letter f with a small x beside it). This opens a window that lets you select the function you want. If this function requires arguments, Excel will prompt you to type them in or select the cells where they are held.

Opposite, we look at an example of how to use a very simple function in order to calculate the odds against winning a lottery draw. On pages 48–49, we will look at some other useful Excel functions.

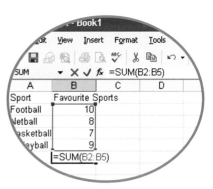

If you've used Excel's SUM function, you will already have explored the basic principles needed to use many of Excel's more powerful commands.

How to apply a function

In this exercise, we use Excel's powerful COMBIN function to work out the odds involved in a lottery draw.

1 In this example, based on the UK National Lottery, we want to calculate the number of possible combinations – in other words, the odds against winning. Start by typing in the text headings shown here.

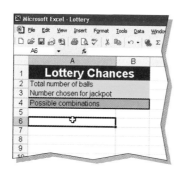

2 Now type in the number of balls in the draw (49) and the number drawn out (6). (You can type in different numbers to suit other lotteries.) Then click on the cell where you want to put the number of possible combinations.

3 We are going to use a function, so click on the Insert Function button which is on the Standard Toolbar.

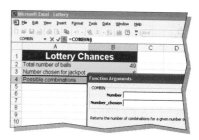

PC TIPS

The COMBIN function can work out many other questions about combinations. For example, imagine that an ice-cream stall has five basic flavours. How many different combinations can be made using just three of the flavours? Excel can quickly tell you: by typing =COMBIN (5,3) you'll instantly find there are 10 different possibilities.

4 In the dialog box that appears, select Math & Trig from the Or select a category list box. Next, select COMBIN from the list under Select a function. The text below tells us that the COMBIN function works out the number of possible combinations, which is just what we want. Click on OK.

5 Excel now brings up a floating window just under the Formula Bar (right). Click on it and drag it down a little (below right) so that you can see the information you've already typed into the worksheet. The COMBIN function has appeared in the cell where we want our answer.

---

6 The window allows us to enter the two arguments that COMBIN uses: Number and Number_chosen. Click on cell B2 (which holds the total number of balls) and you'll see B2 appear in the floating window's first box. It also appears after COMBIN in the cell that will display the answer.

7 Now click on the Number_chosen box in the floating window (top right). The flashing vertical cursor appears there. Click on cell B3, which holds the number chosen (right), and click on the floating window's OK button.

8 In less than a second, Excel works out the total number of possible combinations of six balls chosen from 49 and displays the result – almost 14 million. That means the chance that any single lottery entry will win is nearly 14 million to 1.

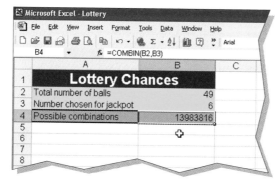

SHORTCUTS

If you've switched off Excel's Formula Bar, you won't be able to see the formulae in the worksheet cells very easily. Select a cell and press [Ctrl]+[`] and you'll instantly be able to see the formula that it contains.

Eight essential Excel functions

W e explored an Excel function properly for the first time on page 47, where we used COMBIN. This is just one of the functions available for carrying out complex calculations, but most are only occasionally useful, and many people rely on the same number of functions over and over again. As you grow more confident you can try more advanced functions, using Excel's Help files to find out how they work. In the meantime, here's our selection of eight of the handiest functions to get you started.

The best way to gain confidence with Excel's functions is to use them. Here's our guide to some functions that will prove handy time and again, plus tips on where to get further information.

● AVERAGE

The AVERAGE function calculates the mean of the numbers in a group of cells. The arguments used by AVERAGE can be a list of cell references, such as A1, B2, C3, D4 or, as in this example, the range of cells B3:B14, which will calculate the average of the numbers in all the cells between B3 and B14. You can also type numbers in directly as arguments – for instance, you could use the formula AVERAGE(2,5,11) to find the average of 2, 5 and 11.

● ROUND

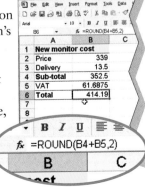

The ROUND function limits the calculation's answer to a set number of digits in cases where it might result in unwanted decimal places. Here, for example, we've used ROUND to ensure that a

financial calculation results in a whole number of pence. The ROUND function needs two arguments: the number you want to round up or down and the maximum number of decimal places you want. You can also use ROUND to produce a whole-number answer by setting the number of digits to zero.

● CONCATENATE

Despite its long name, the CONCATENATE function does a simple job – taking chunks of text and joining them together to make one long line of text. The example opposite shows a common use for CONCATENATE: joining first and last names together to make a full name. The first name is stored in cell B2,

WHAT IT MEANS

MEAN

There are several ways to calculate an average. The one most often used is called the mean. A mean is worked out by adding up a group of numbers and dividing the result by the number of entries in the group. For example, the mean of 2, 5 and 11 is 2+5+11 (=18) divided by 3, which equals 6.

which is used as the first argument. Cell C2 is used as the third argument. In the example (right), we've added a space inside the quotation marks between the two text entries. Excel treats this space as the second argument, placing it between the two names 'Peter' and 'West' so they don't collide.

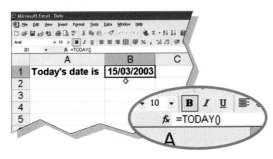

● LOWER

LOWER is a text function that converts all the upper case (capital) letters in text into lower case (small) letters. It requires only one argument – the text to be converted or a reference to the cell that contains that text. The formula in our example ensures that text is consistent, converting both 'WHITE' to 'white' and 'Red' to 'red'. LOWER is a handy way of ensuring that lower case letters are used if the [Caps Lock] key is accidentally pressed.

● TODAY

This function generates a number that represents the current date. The day, month and year are taken from your PC's internal clock, so if this is set incorrectly the result will be wrong. You can apply formatting to the cell in order to control the way in which the date is displayed.

● SUMIF

The SUMIF function adds up the contents of a group of cells – but only if they meet certain, specified conditions. In our example (top right), there are two columns of information – items of expenditure and their cost. We have used SUMIF to pick out all the cells that relate to expenditure on food and then to add them up.

In the formula, the first argument after SUMIF tells Excel where to look for the condition. The second argument shows what to check for, and the third tells Excel where to find the numbers that it has to add up.

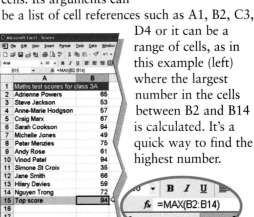

● MAX

MAX finds the largest number in a group of cells. Its arguments can be a list of cell references such as A1, B2, C3, D4 or it can be a range of cells, as in this example (left) where the largest number in the cells between B2 and B14 is calculated. It's a quick way to find the highest number.

● PMT

The PMT (payment) function calculates the cost of loan repayments over a set period at a fixed interest rate. It requires three basic arguments: the interest rate; the number of repayments and the loan's present value.

As this is a very powerful function, you can also add other arguments, perhaps to cater for interest-only loans. In this example, we've used the PMT function to show the monthly repayments for a five-year loan of £9,000. The first argument (E4%/12) provides the monthly percentage interest rate from the annual rate stored in cell E4. The second and third arguments show where the number of repayments and the amount of the loan appear in the table.

Customizing your toolbars

As you become more expert, why not take advantage of the opportunity to set up Excel to suit the way you work?

The two standard toolbars in Excel look very much like the two in Word. This is because all Windows programs – Microsoft products in particular – try to use as many common toolbars and buttons as possible in order to make learning and using software easier.

Not only are Excel toolbars similar to Word's, but you can also change them in the same way. We have already seen how to customize Word's toolbars (see pages 30–33), so let's do the same thing in Excel.

● What you can alter

The main reasons for customizing the Excel toolbars are the same as for Word: to save screen space, to allow commonly used commands to be accessed with a single mouse

The two main Excel toolbars are called Standard and Formatting. As in Word, you can access other, more specific toolbars from the Toolbars option on the View menu, or by clicking on certain buttons on the Standard and Formatting toolbars.

The Standard toolbar commands are very similar to Word's, with Open, Save, Cut, Paste and Print buttons. Options specific to Excel include AutoSum, Sorting and the Chart Wizard. The Formatting toolbar – next to or beneath the Standard toolbar – is also similar to Word's. From here, the typeface size and type can be changed and text can be made bold, underlined or italicized. There are also some formatting options that are particular to Excel. Opposite, we show you how to alter the buttons on either toolbar.

click, and generally to make the program work in a way that suits your specific needs. If, for example, you find you are using a particular option frequently and it's not on the toolbar, you can create a button for it and put it on a toolbar of your choice. You can even create a completely new custom toolbar to replace the existing two.

PC TIPS

Undoing changes

If you make a mistake when customizing toolbars, such as deleting a useful button by mistake, or get carried away and add too many unnecessary new ones, don't worry. You can easily return any toolbar to its original state and simply start again.

To do this, click on the View menu, then click on Toolbars, and select Customize from the commands that appear. The Toolbars tab of the dialog box shows a list of all the toolbars. Select the one you want to return to its original state, and click the Reset button. The toolbar will then be returned to the state it was in when Excel was first installed.

Altering the standard toolbars

You can customize the existing toolbars by removing or adding buttons. We'll practise this on the Standard toolbar.

1 We rarely use the Drawing button in Excel, so we'll remove it for the purposes of this example. Hold down the [Alt] key and drag the Drawing button away from the toolbar with the mouse. You will see a small image of the button move with the mouse pointer; release the mouse button over any part of the worksheet and the Drawing button will disappear from its usual position on the toolbar.

2 A useful button to add is Cycle Font Color. This one-click command lets you change the colour of any text in the worksheet easily and quickly. To add a new button (or to replace one you have previously deleted), go to the View menu and choose Customize at the bottom of the Toolbars sub-menu.

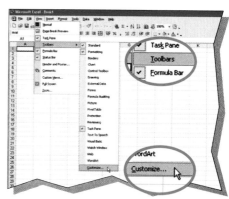

3 Under the Toolbars tab, click on Standard in the Toolbars list. Then select the Commands tab. This will bring up the commands available.

4 First select Format from the Categories menu on the left. Then scroll down the list of the commands and their buttons on the right until you find the one that you want to insert – in this case, the Cycle Font Color button.

5 Click on the button and drag it to the toolbar. A black vertical line will appear on the toolbar to indicate where the button is going to appear.

6 You can also move a button from one toolbar to another, using the [Alt] key as in Step 1. Close the Customize dialog box and then hold down the [Alt] key and click on the Cycle Font Color button you have just placed on the Standard toolbar. Drag it to the Formatting toolbar. Excel knows that you want to move the button rather than delete it, so when you release the mouse the button will automatically move to its new position.

CUSTOM TOOLBARS

You can create your own specialized toolbar by clicking on the New button in the Toolbars section of the Customize dialog box and giving it a name of your choice. Then add new buttons as shown in Steps 2–5.

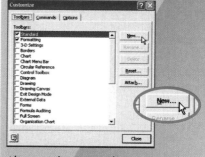

Alternatively, you might want to delete a toolbar you have created and now no longer need. In the Customize dialog box, click on the Toolbars tab. Select the toolbar you want to delete and click on the Delete button. Note that you can only delete new toolbars that you have created; the default toolbars can only be altered or hidden, not deleted.

PC TIPS

In new installations of XP, Excel places both the Standard and Formatting toolbars on the same row. This means that you can rarely see all of the available buttons – especially if you add extra buttons for other commands.

If you prefer, you can tell Excel to display these two toolbars one under the other, as on previous versions of Excel. In the Customize dialog box, click on the Show Standard and Formatting toolbars on two rows option.

7 If you rarely use a toolbar, you might not want it on screen. You cannot delete Excel's toolbars, but you can remove them from view. There are several ways to do this, but the easiest is to untick its name in the list on the Toolbars menu under View.

Working with dates and times

Excel's number-crunching abilities are only part of its power. You can also perform useful calculations on date and time information to solve complicated problems effectively.

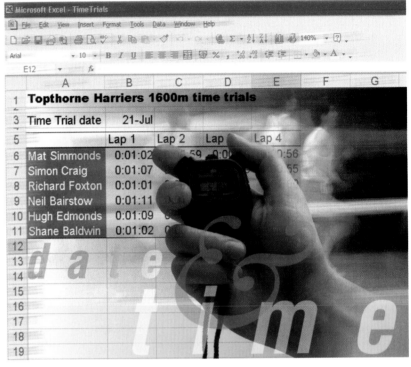

Most of the calculations you do with Excel concern normal numbers: you might use it to tot up the family food budget, keep track of your motoring bills and so on. While these functions are useful, Excel can also help with other types of calculations. Using maths to work on dates and times is one of the easiest ways to get more out of the program.

● A saving grace

If you have a savings account that requires 90 days' notice to make withdrawals, for example, it would be useful to be able to subtract 90 days from the date when you need the money without having to reach for the calendar and count off the days one by one. With Excel, you can type in the date you want to make the withdrawal and simply subtract 90 days from it. Excel knows how many days there are in each month and will give you the right answer almost at once.

Excel can do this because, behind the scenes, it stores all dates as numbers. Whenever you type in a date – 03/02/2004, for example – Excel converts the date to a code number (38020 in this case) which it keeps hidden from view. As a clue to the fact that Excel thinks of the date as a number, notice how the date aligns to the right of a cell, like a number but unlike text.

Once the date is converted to a number, you can use it in calculations. Subtracting 90 from the date you typed in will tell you when you can give notice of withdrawals. Excel subtracts 90 from 38020, and then rapidly converts the numerical answer – 37930 – back into a date, 05/11/2003.

● Times and numbers

It's not only date information that Excel secretly converts into a number; times get the same treatment. Try typing 10:25 into cell A1 of a blank spreadsheet and you'll see that Excel lines it up to the right of the cell – just like a date or number. Now type 4:37 into cell A2 and =A1+A2 into cell A3. When you press the [Enter] key, you'll see that Excel has added the two times and shows 15:02.

Counting days on a calendar is awkward enough but calculations involving hours, minutes and seconds, even with a calculator, are hard. Opposite we'll see how easy it is to do date and time calculations using Excel.

Sometimes date or time calculations can be confusing, but Excel lets you race through them.

PC TIPS

You can tell Excel how you want your date and time information displayed. Highlight the cells and select the Cells command from the Format menu. In the dialog box that appears, select the Number tab and then click on one of the Date or Time categories. The list of Types on the right of the dialog box changes to show you a preview of the formats. Simply choose the one you want and click on the OK button.

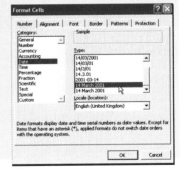

Date and time calculations

In this exercise we show you how to use date and time information in a formula and how to combine it with Excel's other powerful functions.

1 For our example we'll do some date and time calculations on a results sheet for an imaginary school athletics team. Here we've started with a record of the date of the 1600 metres time trial on 21 July, and added four lap times for six athletes. Note that the figures are entered as hours:minutes:seconds.

2 Type in an extra heading for the overall time and, in cell F6, double-click on the AutoSum button to get Excel to add the times in the cells on the left.

3 You'll see the overall time appear, displayed in the same time format. Add formulae for each of the other five athletes.

4 We'll also use some of Excel's functions to save more manual effort. Add an extra row to the table for the best lap time of all the athletes.

5 Into the next cell type =MIN(B6:E11) and press the [Enter] key. Excel uses the MINIMUM function to look through the table of times and displays the lowest (or minimum) time it finds.

WORKING OUT TOTAL TIMES

When working out time calculations, be aware that Excel normally uses a 24-hour clock and rounds down to the nearest day. This is fine if you want to work out what time it will be 11 and a quarter hours after 3:30pm. Just type in 15:30 (3:30pm on a 24-hour clock) and add 11:15. Excel will tell you the answer is 2:45 (or 2:45am) the following day, which is correct. On the other hand, if you want to add 11 and a quarter hours to 15 and a half hours and get the total time elapsed, you need to change the format of the cells (see PC Tips box, opposite). Select Custom in the Category listing and then scroll down the Type list and select [h]:mm:ss – you'll see the correctly formatted answer, 26:45:00, in the Sample section. Click on OK.

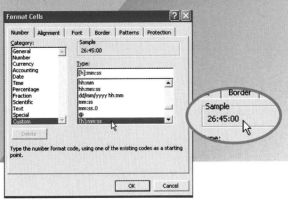

6 Add two more lines: one for the average lap time of all the runners and another one for the slowest lap time. Use =AVERAGE(B6:E11) and =MAX(B6:E11) to calculate the figures.

7 We can also carry out a simple calculation on the date of our time trial. Add a line at the bottom of the table for the date of the next meeting.

8 We want Excel to work out the date four weeks hence: in cell B17, type =B3+28 (note that B3 contains the date we entered in Step 1). Press the [Enter] key and the next date will then appear.

Recording your first Excel macro

You'll often need to repeat the same sequence of commands in Excel to carry out your regular tasks. So why not save time and effort by using macros to teach Excel to do those jobs for you?

Imagine how much time and effort you would save if you could automate everyday chores, such as cooking meals, vacuum-cleaning or doing the laundry. The same could also be said of repetitive tasks in Excel. Wouldn't it be great if you could apply a regularly required piece of formatting, add a frequently used formula or create your favourite type of chart with a single click of the mouse button or a keyboard shortcut?

The good news is that there is a way you can teach Excel to do the jobs you have to perform often – by creating a macro. Once Excel knows what to do, it will do it for you automatically, at the click of a mouse, time after time.

● What is a macro?
A macro is a saved sequence of actions linked together to perform a particular task. The easiest way to create a macro is to record one. All you have to do is start up Excel's built-in Macro Recorder and show it the sequence of actions in the job you want it to remember.

The Macro Recorder memorizes these actions in much the same way as a person watching you cook might write down a list of the steps you perform to prepare a dish. You only have to run through the steps once and Excel will record the exact sequence and be ready to repeat it whenever you want.

● Name that macro
When you record a macro, Excel asks you to name it and gives you the option of typing in a brief description of what it does. It's wise to choose a meaningful name that you'll be able to remember in the future and to take advantage of the opportunity to provide the description in case, in a few months time, you forget the purpose of your macro.

Excel also gives you the chance to set up a keyboard shortcut for your macro. If you do this, you'll be able to run your macro just by pressing the [Ctrl] key and another key simultaneously. However, Excel already uses a number of keyboard shortcuts so you should

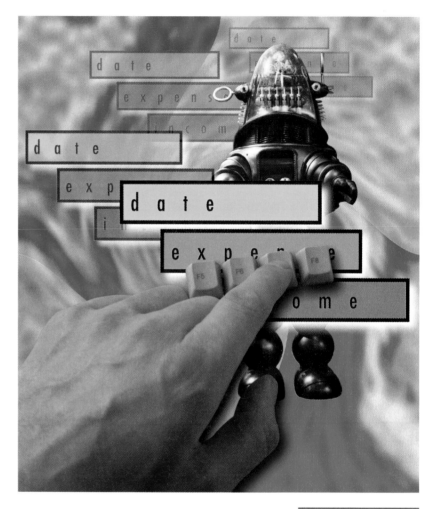

choose a key that isn't already in use. To see a list of what's taken, search for 'shortcut key' in Excel's Help file.

You can still run your macro, even if you decide not to set up a keyboard shortcut. All you have to do is select the Macros option from the Tools menu's Macro sub-menu to view the Macros dialog box. This will give you access to all the macros you have recorded. Then just highlight the macro you want to use and click on the Run button to play it.

Opposite, we show you how to apply several formatting commands with a single action. We'll then show you how to create even more powerful macros that will save you repeating the same actions time and again.

Recording an Excel macro

Here we use a macro to apply labour-intensive cell formatting. Like any macro, once recorded, it can be used with any Excel workbook you start in the future.

1 We've already learnt how to apply formatting to a cell by using the buttons on Excel's Formatting toolbar (see Stage 1, pages 58–59). Here we've changed the font, the font size and colour, the cell background colour and made the text bold. However, this process has taken several clicks of the mouse to do it.

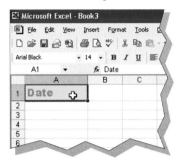

2 It would be much more convenient to use a simple keyboard shortcut to apply this formatting regularly. Let's use Excel's Macro Recorder to record the steps we use to apply the formatting. Select Macro from the Tools menu and choose Record New Macro from the sub-menu that appears.

3 Next, fill in some details about your macro. Type a meaningful name into the Macro name text box. Then type a description of what the macro does into the Description text box. It's important to do both of these so that you can check what the macro is used for in the future if you forget.

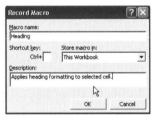

4 Now you need to decide what keyboard shortcut you want to use to run the macro. Be careful to choose a key that isn't already used for something else, such as a shortcut for a command on one of Excel's menus or for a macro you've already recorded. We've typed an [m] into the Shortcut key box. Click on OK.

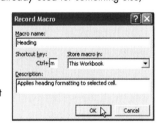

5 Excel starts the Macro Recorder and displays this small toolbar. From now on, every action you perform is recorded as a part of your macro.

6 Now work through the steps you would usually take to apply the formatting you want to the selected cell. Use any of Excel's cell formatting commands: colour, font size, bold, italics and so on.

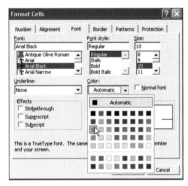

7 Notice how the status bar at the bottom of the Excel window reminds you that the Macro Recorder is recording.

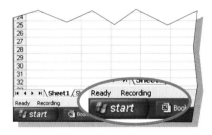

PC TIPS

Sometimes you might find it useful to stop a macro while it is running – perhaps because you started it accidentally or because you have applied it to the wrong cell. All you need to do to stop a macro before it completes its actions is press the [Esc] key.

8 When you have completed all the steps, click on the Stop Recording button on the Macro Recorder toolbar (it's the button marked with a small, dark blue square).

9 The quickest way to run your macro is to highlight the cells you want to format and press [Ctrl]+[m] together. Here we've selected two cells and added the formatting to both at once.

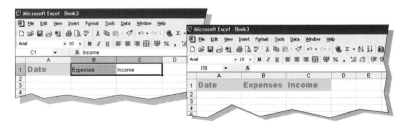

Macros and cell referencing

Your Excel macros may need to refer to particular cells in your spreadsheets. Here's a way to avoid any confusion between absolute and relative cell referencing.

Both absolute and relative cell references can be used to send data exactly where you want to send it – automatically.

We've already seen how to use macros to get Excel to perform frequently repeated tasks (see pages 54–55). The process starts with you recording the individual steps that make up the task. You can then save them as a macro, giving it a name as well as a keyboard shortcut, which allows you to play it back whenever required.

Recording and playing macros in Excel uses the same process as in most Office programs. However, there is one important difference – the extra complication of the choice between absolute and relative cell addressing (see Stage 3, pages 62–63).

● Absolute and relative referencing

Absolute and relative cell references are the two ways you can tell Excel which cell you want it to work on. If you think of these in terms of street directions, for example, you can quickly see the difference.

A direction such as 'Go to the police station and the hospital is directly opposite' is an absolute address: no matter where you are it works – as long as you know how to find the police station! However, 'Turn left and then take the second turning on the right to reach the hospital' is a relative address – it works only from your current position. If you try it from other locations it is useless.

Just as each set of directions has its place, so Excel's absolute and relative cell addressing allow you to create formulae and macros that are right for the task in hand.

● The right choice

It's important to be certain which sort of cell referencing you want to use, or you could end up with some unexpected results. For example, suppose cell B2 is selected and you record a macro that refers to cell A1 with relative, instead of absolute, addressing. When you play the macro it will not refer to the cell that you intended.

Excel's Macro Recorder toolbar includes a button that you can use to tell Excel whether you want to work with absolute or relative cell referencing. On the next page, we'll show you how you can use this to help record similar macros for moving cell data – one to move the data to an absolute position in the worksheet, and another to move the data up by a row and left by a column.

Recording relative and absolute macros

To begin with, we'll set up a macro that copies data to a cell at a point near to the one you are working on. Then we'll create a second macro that always sends data to a particular point on the worksheet.

1 Start with a new worksheet and type a single word, 'Balance', into cell B2. We'll move this word around our worksheet to demonstrate how to use macros with relative and absolute cell referencing.

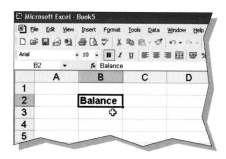

2 Bring up the Record Macro dialog box through the Macro section of the Tools menu (see pages 54–55). When the box appears, type in 'relmove' for the name (short for relative move), 'q' for the Shortcut key, and a brief description.

PC TIPS

Sharing Macros

Macros are usually just saved for use with the worksheet where they are recorded. If you record a very useful macro you can use it in other worksheets. Just select Personal Macro Workbook from the Store macro in option in the Record Macro dialog box.

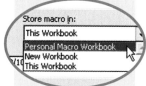

3 The Macro toolbar appears. Press the Relative Reference button and then press [Ctrl]+[X] to cut the cell contents from cell B2.

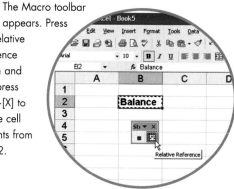

4 Click on cell A1 and press [Ctrl]+[V] to paste the cell contents. Then click on the Stop Recording button.

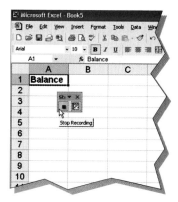

5 Next we'll repeat the process – with a difference: move 'Balance' back to cell B2 and bring up the Record Macro dialog box as you did earlier. Next, name the macro 'absmove' (for absolute move) and type 'n' into the Shortcut key. Finally, type in your new description in case you forget its purpose.

6 Press the Relative Reference button again to turn it off. Then press [Ctrl]+[X] to cut the cell contents from cell B2, click on cell A1 and press [Ctrl]+[V] to paste 'Balance' again. Then click on the Stop Recording button.

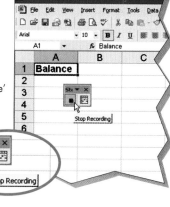

7 Delete the contents of all the cells in the worksheet and type 'Income' into cell C3. Press [Ctrl]+[q] while C3 is still selected. This is the shortcut for 'relmove'. You'll see that instead of being copied to the top-left cell (A1), 'Income' is copied to B2 – one cell up and to the left of its original place – exactly the same relative position as the move you made in Steps 3 and 4.

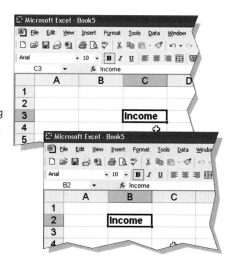

8 Repeat Step 7, but this time press [Ctrl]+[n], the shortcut for 'absmove'. You'll see that 'Income' is copied to the top left cell. That's because this macro uses an absolute cell reference to A1. No matter where the current cell is in your worksheet, pressing [Ctrl]+[n] will always copy it to cell A1. Finally, save your new worksheet.

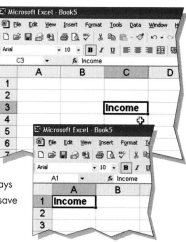

Tips for recording and playing macros

Experienced Excel users employ many clever little tricks to make recording and playing macros much easier. Here are some expert tips to help you master macros.

We covered how to record and play macros on pages 54–55 and explained how to avoid confusion between absolute and relative cell referencing on pages 56–57. This time, we want to give you some ideas that will help you to record and play macros more efficiently. We also include some tips on how to avoid the pitfalls you might encounter. Most of the advice is pure common sense and really just involves planning what you want to do in advance.

● Rehearse the steps of your macro

Once you've decided that you need to record a macro, the best thing to do is plan out all the steps that will make it up. It's a good idea to list the sequence of steps on paper. Then, practise doing them a couple of times without starting the Macro Recorder so that you're confident you know all the steps by heart. You should then be able to record your macro perfectly on the first attempt.

● Work around mouse actions you can't record

Excel's Macro Recorder can't record all the mouse movements and clicks you make. The computer will beep to warn you if this happens while you are recording a macro. Don't worry though, because you can use the keyboard's cursor keys to do many of the

mouse actions that aren't recognized by the Macro Recorder. So, if you hear a beep, try the action again using the keyboard.

● Save before you play a new macro

Once you've recorded and saved a new macro, don't rush into playing it straightaway, because you can't use the Undo command to reverse the effects of a macro. Instead, save your worksheet and then play your macro to see if it behaves as you intended. This way is much safer because, if things go wrong, you can close the worksheet without saving the changes the macro has made and you will be able to start again.

Once you are happy with the macro, you can add a button for it to Excel's toolbar. This gives you one-click access to the macro. We show you how to do this opposite.

● Keep the Macro Toolbar out of the way

If you're recording a long, complex macro, it can be easier if you move the Macro Recorder toolbar right out of your way so that you can see everything clearly. This won't affect the macro at all. Simply click on the Macro Recorder toolbar and drag and drop it where you like.

Once you've created a macro, you can allocate a button for it on the toolbar.

Adding a macro toolbar button

For quicker access to a useful macro, why not add a button to your Excel toolbar? Here's how to add and customize a button for any of your macros.

1 Start Excel and open the worksheet that you used to create your macros (see pages 56–57). Bring up the Customize dialog box by selecting Customize from the Tools menu.

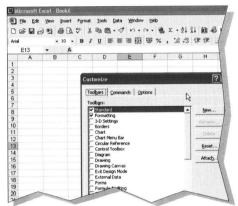

2 Click on the Commands tab and scroll down the Categories list until you see the Macros entry. Click on it and you'll see the list of Commands on the right change.

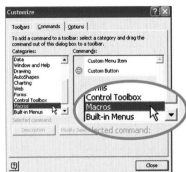

3 Click on the Custom Button command and drag it onto one of Excel's toolbars (right). You'll see a vertical bar appear; release the mouse button when this bar is in the right place. Your button will appear as a smiling face (far right).

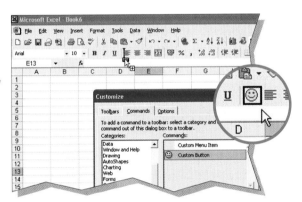

4 Right-click on your new button. In the Name section of the menu that appears, enter a description of what it does (this appears when the mouse passes over your new button). Here we've typed 'Move to top left cell'.

5 Now click on the Assign Macro command from the same menu. When the Assign Macro dialog box pops up, click on the absmove macro and then on the OK button. Don't close the Customize dialog box.

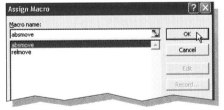

6 Let's change our button icon to one that suits our macro. Right-click on the button to bring up the menu and then select the Edit Button Image command.

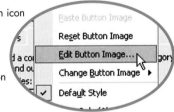

7 The Button Editor is like a tiny paint program – you can edit the button image dot by dot. Press the Clear button to remove the smiling face.

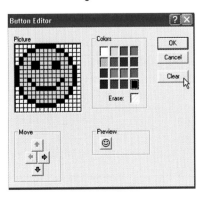

8 Paint your image by clicking on a colour and then clicking on the dots. We've gone for an image that visually explains the button's function.

9 When you've finished your image, click on the OK button and close the Customize dialog box. Your personalized button and its label will now appear on the toolbar and work just like any of Excel's normal buttons.

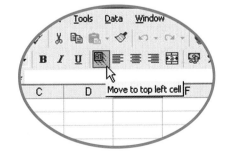

Microsoft® Excel

Adding a background

You can liven up even the least interesting set of figures in a worksheet by adding an appropriate picture to the background.

Excel's formatting tools, which include typefaces, font sizes and cell background colours, are invaluable for making worksheet information stand out (see Stage 1, pages 58–59).

We've also seen that adding a picture to the chart's bars or segments produces a much more original and interesting look (see Stage 3, pages 66–67). To help lift even the most flat and boring worksheet, you can go even further and add a background picture to the entire worksheet.

● **Background information**
A background picture works rather like the image you can add to the Windows Desktop (see Stage 3, pages 12–13). The picture you choose lies behind the information in the worksheet, just as the image on your Windows Desktop lies behind the icons.

Not all worksheets actually merit a picture background: accountants are unlikely to add a picture to an annual budget, for example. However, Excel's grid-based structure makes it perfect for less formal documents, such as an athletics results sheet (see page 53). Many worksheets with a relatively low level of information in their cells present an ideal opportunity for a picture background.

Adding a picture as a background to a worksheet is easy; the most difficult aspect is

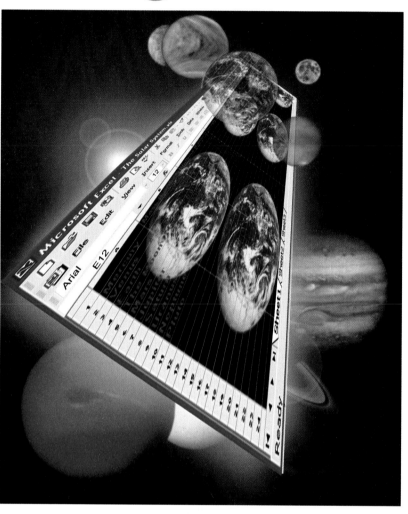

choosing the right kind of picture. In order to be able to read the text and numbers in your worksheet clearly, you need to make sure that the colours in the picture contrast with the colour of your text.

Busy and very colourful pictures can often prove difficult to work with. If the picture you want to use makes the information in the worksheet difficult to read, you have several options. The first is to choose text colours and typefaces that will aid legibility, such as heavy, bold typefaces. You can also try using a graphics program such as PHOTO-PAINT that will decrease the brightness and/or contrast of the picture.

Finally, try adding background colours to those cells that contain information. The picture will still show through, but adding a cell colour obscures the cell's background and ensures the text in the cell is legible.

It's easy to give an extra dimension to your Excel worksheets by adding a picture to the background. We show you how to explore the options on the next page.

TILING PICTURES

Background pictures in Excel are tiled. That means that pictures are repeated horizontally and vertically to fill the worksheet – just like tiles on a bathroom wall. Some pictures work better than others when tiled; in particular, you'll probably want to avoid distracting edges where tiles meet. To avoid the unattractive sight of poorly matched tile edges, look carefully for pictures that tile seamlessly so that the join between them is completely invisible.

Adding a picture background

Picture backgrounds can be used to enhance any type of Excel document.

1 Here's a worksheet containing homework about the solar system. We could give some of the cells background colours, but instead we'll experiment with a space theme to spice up the worksheet's appearance.

2 Click on the Format menu, select Sheet and click on the Background option in the sub-menu.

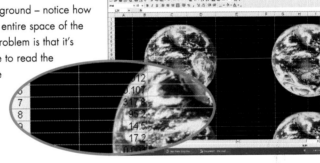

Microsoft® Excel

3 This will open the Sheet Background dialog box so that you can choose the picture you want to use.

Locate the picture (we've used a clip-art picture from a CD-ROM) and then click on the Insert button.

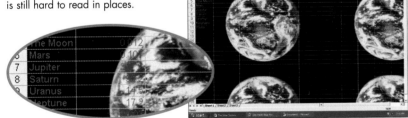

4 Here's the worksheet with the Earth background – notice how it's tiled to fill the entire space of the worksheet. The problem is that it's almost impossible to read the information in the worksheet's cells because it's in black text in unfilled cells.

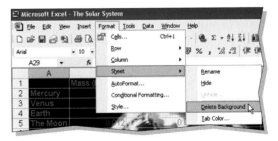

5 To solve this problem, we've tried changing the colour of the text to magenta. It helps, but the text is still hard to read in places.

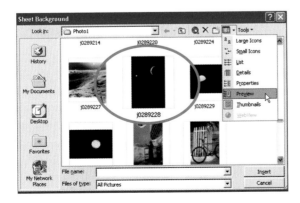

6 Try experimenting with different backgrounds to optimize legibility. Remove the current background by selecting Delete Background from the Sheet sub-menu.

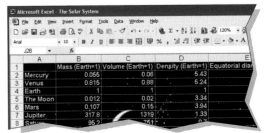

7 Now open the Sheet Background dialog box, as in Step 2, and look through some other pictures. To get a larger preview of the image you select, choose Preview from the drop-down Views menu.

8 This picture of the moon and stars is better as it has less background detail than the previous image. In addition, by making the text bold and bright yellow, it has become easily legible.

Simple cell naming

Excel's cell references, such as A1, B6 and ZZ193, can be hard to remember. Avoid taxing your memory by giving these cells recognizable names.

Almost everything you do with Excel involves working with cells in worksheets. Up until now we have always talked about cells in terms of their alpha-numeric references, or co-ordinates. For example, A1 is the top left cell of a worksheet. Though alpha-numeric cell references are convenient to start with, they aren't very user friendly.

A few days or weeks after you've created a worksheet stuffed full of cell references, it can be hard to remember which cells hold which bits of information. For example, to work out exactly what's going on with the formula =(C1/D4)*G2 you need to look back at each of the cells mentioned to see exactly what information they represent. A formula, such as =(Distance/FuelEconomy)*PetrolCost would be much more useful. Fortunately, Excel is as adept at working with names as it is with cell references. All you need to do is give your cells relevant names.

● Naming names

Cell names can be as obvious as you like, from 'JanExp' to 'January_Expenses'. Full-length names are easier to remember, but the shortened form is quicker to type (especially if typed into a lot of cells) and is almost as easy to understand.

There's an extra advantage to working with names rather than cell references. Anyone who needs to use your worksheet can understand it

more quickly. This is of benefit to business users who share worksheet files with their colleagues over a network, but it can also help introduce worksheets to your family, who might find it difficult to work with algebraic formulae.

The only catch with naming is that it can take time to highlight and name all the important cells in your worksheet.

● Automatic naming

To save you lots of time and repetitive work, Excel provides a way of identifying cells automatically using information you've already typed in. For example, in many of our Excel exercises we've given the worksheet rows and columns labels such as 'Expenses' or 'Sales'. Excel can use these row and column labels to refer to all the cells in a rectangular area automatically.

Let's imagine that you have a worksheet with a table of months, January through to December, listed along the top; your expense items, such as Groceries, Bills and Savings, are down the left side; and your numbers are inside the worksheet to represent the amount spent on each item for each month.

Each cell of data automatically gets a special name, which is made up of the column label and the row label. If, for example, column D had the label 'January' and row 10 had the label 'Groceries,' then you are able to refer to cell D10 simply as 'January Groceries'.

Using names in cells as part of a formula can make worksheets easier for people to use both at home and at work.

Working with cell names and labels

To avoid confusion in the future when adding to, or otherwise altering, a worksheet, make the most of Excel's ability to create formulae using easy-to-understand cell names.

1 Here's a worksheet for recording monthly household expenses. Instead of using formulae with cell references to add up the monthly totals, we'll use names as an alternative.

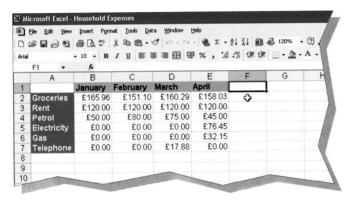

2 It would be time-consuming to name each of the 24 individual cells. Instead, let's take advantage of the fact that we've already typed labels for the rows (Groceries, Rent, Telephone and so forth) and columns (January to April). Highlight all the cells containing information and then select Name from the Insert menu. Choose Create from the sub-menu that appears.

3 Now Excel will open the Create Names dialog box. Excel makes an educated guess at the names to use: if there aren't already ticks in the Top row and Left column boxes, click them to make ticks appear. This tells Excel to use the text in the top row and left column as names. Click on the OK button.

4 To add a total for the month of January, click on cell B8 and type =SUM(January), then press the [Enter] key. Repeat the process for cells C8, D8 and E8.

PC TIPS

Checking your cell names

For a reminder of which names refer to which cells, use the Define Name dialog box. To bring this up, click on the Insert menu, Name and then Define.

5 We'll name cell B8 manually: click on cell B8 and then click on the Name text box just to the left of the Formula Bar. Now type in a name (Jan_total) and press the [Enter] key.

6 Repeat this exercise for the February, March and April totals (cells C8, D8 and E8) using the names Feb_total, Mar_total and Apr_total.

7 Now let's use cell F8 to add up a grand total for the four months. Click on the cell and type =SUM(Jan_total:Apr_total). This is a much friendlier formula than its cell reference equivalent, =SUM(B8:E8).

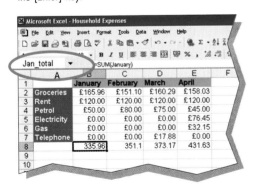

8 Press the [Enter] key and Excel will look up the cell names you entered in Steps 5 and 6, and work out the calculation just as it does with cell references.

Keeping work secret

If you want to keep workbooks on your computer hidden from prying eyes – or if you want to stop anyone else inadvertently (or deliberately) making changes to an important Excel document – why not use your own secret passwords to protect them?

I f you share a PC at home, you might create documents you don't want others to see. It would be such a shame, for instance, if somebody accidentally opened your top secret list of Christmas presents. Similarly, you might not want other members of your family worrying over the intimate details of the family finances by discovering just how much you splashed out on that holiday for them.

● Personal files

By far the most secure method of keeping personal files private is to set up separate accounts under Windows XP (see Stage 2, pages 18–19). Not all families like to use such a strict approach though, and instead simply use personal folders within the My Documents folder. However, this doesn't make the documents secure. Anyone who wants to pry will know exactly which documents they need to open to find out secrets. Alternatively, you could keep sensitive documents only on floppy disks, which you could keep locked up

Excel can act as a sentry by denying access to a workbook unless the user enters the correct password.

in a safe place. This is certainly more secure, but it would be annoying to have to insert disks every time you want to work on your files – and the chances of losing or damaging a disk are high. It is also easy to forget to delete the copy from the hard disk after working on the document.

● The foolproof method

If you don't want to use Windows XP's accounts feature, the next most secure solution is to add a password to your Excel workbook. This is a simple procedure, which effectively makes it impossible for anyone who does not know the password to open up the workbook and view the contents.

Using passwords

Protecting your Excel documents with a secret password is simple; the hardest part is choosing the password itself.

PC TIPS

Passwords not only prevent others from opening a protected file, but can also prevent files from being altered by unauthorized people. This is useful when the file holds information that others need to know but that you do not want changed – except by yourself.

Anyone who wants to make changes must supply the password. Those who don't know it can open the workbook but in Read-Only form. This means that they can view it but any alterations they make to it cannot be saved. You can

create such a set-up by using the Password to modify option in the Save Options dialog box (above), rather than the Password to open text box. Now, when the file is opened, only those knowing the password can make changes to the workbook.

1 Open the Excel workbook that you want to password protect. Here, we've chosen to keep a list of Christmas presents secret. Choose Save As from the File menu.

2 From the Save As dialog box, click on Tools and then select General Options from the drop-down menu that appears at the far right.

3 A Save Options dialog box will then open. The cursor will be blinking in the Password to open text box ready for your entry (ignore the other options for now).

4 Type in the word you have chosen. You will see that asterisks appear instead of the letters; this ensures that anyone else looking at your screen can't see it as you type it for the first time. When you have finished, click on OK.

5 The Confirm Password dialog box will appear. Excel asks you to type in the password again. This is done to make sure that you spelt your password correctly the first time.

6 Type in the password again, exactly as you did before, and then click on OK. The dialog box warns you that passwords are 'case-sensitive' – that means it matters whether you use small or capital letters. If you get it wrong, Excel takes you back to step 5 to start again.

> Caution: If you lose or forget the password, it cannot be recovered. It is advisable to keep a list of passwords and their corresponding workbook and sheet names in a safe place. (Remember that passwords are case-sensitive.)

7 The Save As dialog box reappears. Click on Save to save the workbook together with the password.

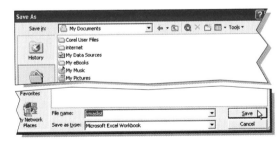

8 Since you're saving the workbook with the original name, a dialog box asks if you want to replace the existing 'xmaslist.xls' file. Click on the Yes button to continue. Note: as soon as you click on the Yes button and save over the existing version of this file, there's no way to go back to the old, non-protected workbook, so you must choose memorable passwords.

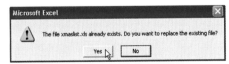

9 To see what effect password protection has, close the workbook and then try to open it again. You will find that, instead of the file opening immediately, Excel will show you a Password dialog box. To open the workbook and work on the worksheet as normal, you need to type in the password and click on OK.

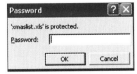

10 If the password is typed incorrectly a warning box appears (below). The password must be spelt correctly, and with the same capitalization as you typed in steps 4 and 6, in order for the worksheet to be accessed. Excel will warn you if you make a mistake.

Lining up and spacing objects

Placing objects in a perfectly straight line with exactly the right amount of space between them can be infuriatingly difficult if you are forced to rely on your own judgement. But CorelDRAW can help you get things exactly right.

Creating a repetitive pattern or a picture consisting of identical elements – such as a row of terraced houses – is simple in CorelDRAW. All you have to do to produce a series of duplicated images is to use the Copy and Paste functions. However, if you need to line up a series of images accurately or space them out evenly, this can be a tricky, time-consuming job.

Fortunately, CorelDRAW can do this for you as well, thanks to the Align and Distribute function. This will ensure that any objects you select line up exactly in relation to one another and appear precisely where you want them. CorelDRAW also has a useful built-in grid to guide you in positioning them.

● **Aligning objects**
Using the Align options, you can choose to line up images horizontally or vertically. You also have the choice of aligning them along whichever 'edge' you specify. For example, if you create a row of houses, you will want them all to line up at their base, but a row of stalactites would look better aligned at the top.

You can even align objects from their centre. This might not seem very useful, but, as we show on page 68, you can use this option to place a series of objects on top of one another. We show how to use it to produce a pattern of concentric circles which resembles an archery target. In our example, the circles end up on top of the largest circle in descending order of size, thus producing the target effect.

Finally, instead of aligning objects against a common edge, you can choose to line them up against a specified image or target object. This is useful when you want to organize elements that have an irregular shape and size.

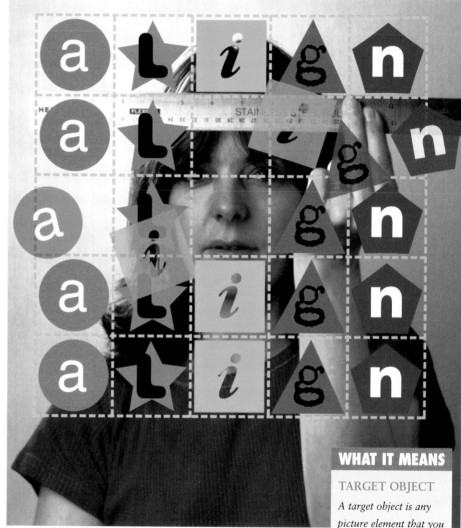

● **Distributing objects**
The spacing between objects is controlled by the Distribute options, which allow you to space elements evenly within a designated area or around a specified image.

Although you might not need this option as often as Align, it can still be very useful. Many picture elements are based on a series of repeated objects with regular spacing between them, such as the garden fence design used as an example on page 69.

WHAT IT MEANS

TARGET OBJECT
A target object is any picture element that you specify as the reference point for positioning other objects. It will be set automatically if you select several shapes together (by pressing the [Shift] key while you click on them). The target object is the last one that you select.

To space the fence posts, you need only position the extreme left- and right-hand ones accurately. The remaining posts can then be evenly distributed in between. By choosing the target object and distribution carefully, you can create a design where elements are spaced at equal distances from any image – a task which would be very awkward and time-consuming by hand.

● Flexible controls

The Align and Distribute function is available either from the Arrange menu or directly from the Property bar after more than one object has been selected with the Pick Tool. The controls for both functions also include Preview buttons, which allow you to see what a design looks like before you decide whether

to use it, and a Reset button in case you don't like the result. This is useful when positioning a large number of objects, as the results can be difficult to predict. As both tools are easy to experiment with, Preview means that you can try out various options without ruining your previous picture.

Follow the examples on the next two pages and then try out some of your own ideas. Soon you will have mastered how to space objects with precision – and you will wonder how designers coped without CorelDRAW's Align and Distribute functions.

● Positioning on a grid

CorelDRAW also offers handy shortcuts. In the examples discussed above, the reference points used for alignment and distribution are all elements of the drawing. But you can just as easily position objects by reference to a point on the screen. To help you with positioning, CorelDRAW can display a grid on screen (see Using the grid, below). Instead of having to place objects precisely, you can click on the Snap To Grid button, which will automatically align them with whichever grid point is nearest when you let go of the object.

Using the grid

CorelDRAW can provide you with a grid of regularly spaced lines to give you a visual reference for positioning objects on the page.

1 One very simple way to position objects on a page is to use the rulers at the top and left-hand side of the screen. However, to ensure that objects line up accurately in relation to one another, it is better to use CorelDRAW's grid.

2 Click on View and choose Grid from the drop-down menu. A grid of grey lines will then appear on screen. This will help you to see how each element lines up on the page.

3 To help you position the objects accurately over the grid, click on the Snap To Grid button.

4 Now, whenever you move an object with the Pick Tool, the normally invisible box around it will automatically 'click' into place over the nearest intersection of the lines. Here, we are using this to align the four stars exactly.

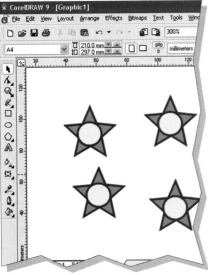

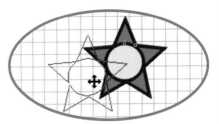

Experimenting with alignment

Although alignment is often used to position objects in a straight line (see opposite), it allows you to do much more. Here we see how to place six circles on top of one another.

1 Start by drawing half a dozen circles, each slightly smaller than the one before. Fill each circle with a different colour so that you will be able to see what happens when they overlap (see Stage 2, page 71). You don't need to worry about placing them exactly.

2 Select the Pick Tool from the toolbox and drag it across an area that completely encompasses the circles on your page. You'll see a single set of selection handles appear around your shapes (below). If any shape is left outside this area, try again.

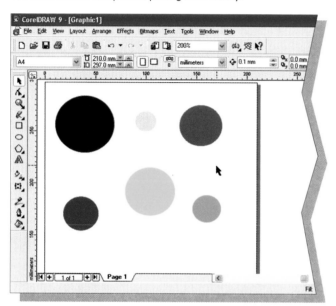

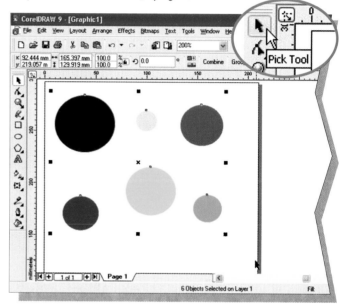

3 Click on the Arrange menu and then select Align and Distribute from the drop-down menu.

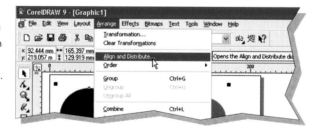

S H O R T C U T S

CorelDRAW offers a number of time-saving keyboard commands. If you press the [C] and then the [E] key after selecting the circles in Step 2, CorelDRAW aligns them without having to use the Align and Distribute dialog box at all.

4 The dialog box that pops up has two tabs. Select the Align tab and then the Center option for both horizontal alignment (at the top of the dialog box) and vertical alignment (on the left of the dialog box). Click on the Preview button.

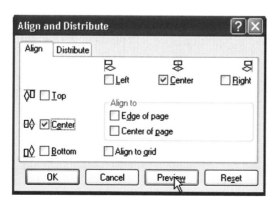

5 You'll see that all the circles move on top of each other. They are arranged with the largest at the back and the smallest at the front because that is the order you drew them in Step 1. All the circles are aligned perfectly, in a way that would be very time-consuming and almost impossible to do so accurately by hand. Click on OK to keep this arrangement.

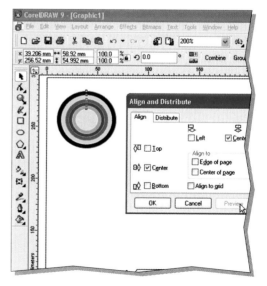

Using distribution

In this example, we will use Alignment and Distribution to create a regularly spaced picket fence to use as a logo.

1 Start by drawing a single fence post. We've used a simple rectangle and then put a spike on top by adding an extra node to this edge (see Stage 3, page 73).

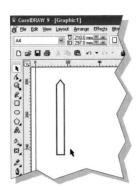

2 Copy and paste the fence post several times, and then position the posts very roughly at the top of the page.

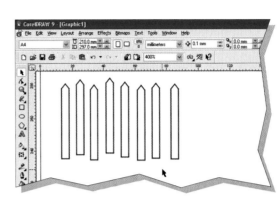

3 First we need to line up the posts. Follow Step 3 on the previous page to bring up the Align and Distribute dialog box, and select the Align tab. This time, tick the Bottom option from the vertical alignments on the left. Then click on OK.

4 This has moved the posts so that they now all line up at the bottom, but the horizontal spacing is still variable.

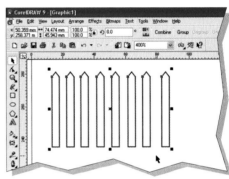

5 Bring up the Align and Distribute dialog box once more, and this time click on the Distribute tab.

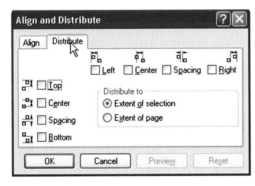

6 The top line of options controls the objects' horizontal distribution. Select the Center option. The Extent of selection setting beneath these options means that the objects will be spaced evenly between the two outermost objects. Leave this checked and click on OK.

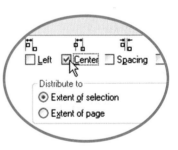

7 You'll now see that CorelDRAW has moved the fence posts so that they are equally spaced. Once again, a few simple mouse clicks have saved an awful lot of trial-and-error positioning.

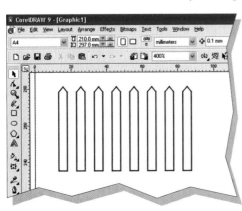

8 Finally, we've added two rails as horizontal rectangles behind the posts (for instructions on how to set one image behind another, see Stage 2, page 71) and some text to finish off our logo.

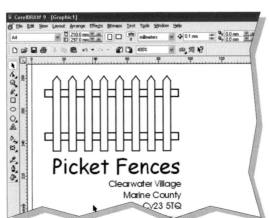

PC TIPS

Once you have finished aligning and distributing your collection of objects, you will need to protect the arrangement from accidental changes when you are moving it.

Usually you will want to move the image as a whole, so group the items after you've positioned them. To do this, press [Ctrl]+[G] while the items are still selected. This shortcut groups the items so that you can move them together (see Stage 2, pages 80–81).

Advanced curves and nodes

One of the most powerful drawing features – the bezier curve – is also one of the hardest to master. Here's how to control curves and nodes in your drawings.

Changing the shape of objects in a drawing is a fundamental skill for computer artists who want to create artwork that goes beyond rectangles, ellipses or lines. As we've already seen (Stage 2, pages 76–77), working with bezier curves lets you turn the simplest objects – rectangles – into far more complex shapes.

Almost any object in CorelDRAW can be turned into bezier curves. Even individual letters in a word or phrase can be reshaped to suit your artwork (Stage 3, pages 72–73). With a few movements of the mouse, nodes on the curve can be moved and the shape of a line or object changed beyond recognition.

● Bezier basics

The basic principle of adding and dragging nodes is easy to understand. You can think of the outline of a shape or line as if it was made of infinitely stretchy elastic. For example, think of a square as a collection of four regularly spaced pins holding a stretched elastic band against a backboard. The lines are perfectly straight from one pin to another.

Converting the square into curves (see Curves and lines box, page 71) allows you to reposition the individual pins; the elastic simply follows suit. You can also add extra pins – or nodes – to the elastic band, dragging them anywhere on the backboard. The first extra pin turns the square into a pentagon; the next turns it into a hexagon and so on. You can also drag nodes inwards to create star shapes.

● Beyond straight lines

This pin-plus-elastic analogy holds up perfectly until you add real curves to your shape. For example, you can transform a square into an arch by making the top-most edge into a smooth and symmetrical bezier curve. But there's no direct parallel for bezier curves in either the real world of art or elastic – they exist only in the virtual art studio.

The reason is that, behind the scenes, CorelDRAW is using mathematical formulae to plot the path of each curve. Bezier curves are named after Pierre Bezier, a French engineer who discovered a powerful way to represent all manner of smooth and sharp curves with relatively simple formulae. The beauty of CorelDRAW is that you can use these formulae without knowing anything at all about the underlying maths.

In order to control the path of a bezier curve, you just need to learn how to control the small 'handles' on the nodes. These handles are known as control points and you'll find one on every node on the curve (see Segments and nodes, page 71). They aren't complicated to use – CorelDRAW does the maths for you and redraws the line whenever you move one of the control points.

CorelDRAW's Convert To Curves command allows you to create any shape you want – just start off with a basic square and then transform it.

CURVES AND LINES

Art software often refers to straight lines and edges as curves which can cause confusion. This seems nonsensical to many people, but the software's logic is that any shape becomes a curve as soon as you use the Convert To Curves command on it. The shape's outline itself won't change, but the software now allows you to alter the nodes that define its shape.

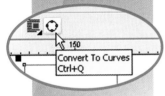

● Unpredictable maths

Although the maths is done by CorelDRAW, there's still a knack to controlling curves. Many CorelDRAW novices, who find it easy to get started with nodes and shapes, find bezier curves difficult to master. Accidentally moving the wrong handle can result in your line or shape curving in the wrong direction. It's this initial unpredictability that deters many people from getting the most out of bezier curves.

The trick to mastering these curves is to look more closely at how CorelDRAW splits a curve into segments, nodes and control points. Of these, the control points tend to be the most difficult to understand – partly because in a finished drawing, all of the control points are invisible. For example, almost all of the images supplied on the CorelDRAW CD-ROM use control points on the shapes and curves that make up the overall picture – you just can't see them.

In order to see the individual curves and shapes, you must dissemble the picture using the Ungroup command and then use the Shape Tool to view the control points for the individual nodes. When you drag these control points around, you will find that you can make dramatic changes to the shapes with small movements of the mouse.

In the exercises on the following pages, we show how to zoom in and fine-tune each of these elements in your own drawings. The same principles apply whether you draw regular lines or shapes and tweak their segments, nodes and control points (see page 72), or whether you draw your curves freehand (see page 73).

● Experiment with tracing

Bezier curves are a very abstract aspect of art, and therefore it can be daunting to sit down with a blank page and begin to practise. However, one very effective way to learn how to create curves and shapes that appear natural and flowing is tracing (see pages 90–91). If you open an existing CorelDRAW picture or a photo, you can overlay bezier curves and shapes on it, without needing to stretch your own skills. Add and edit as many nodes as you need to follow the forms in the underlying image.

Segments and nodes

In order to convert a shape into curves, CorelDRAW splits it up into segments and nodes.

When you are working with a shape that has been converted to curves, it is important to understand that CorelDRAW divides it into segments. The segments are indicated by the nodes that you can see when you use the Shape Tool; each segment will have a node at either end. The simplest shape is a straight line with two nodes – by moving these two nodes you can change the position and length of the line.

CorelDRAW lets you turn any segment of a line or shape into an actual curve (see below). It adds control points – small handles that control the path of the line between any two nodes – and moving these allows you to 'bend' the line. By thinking of a shape or line as a collection of segments which have independent control over the path of the line between each node, you'll soon master curves in CorelDRAW.

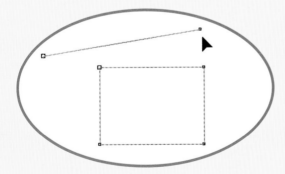

In CorelDRAW, a straight line can be a 'curve'. It has just one segment, with a node at each end. A square that has been converted to curves is a four-segment, four-node shape where two segments are joined together at each corner.

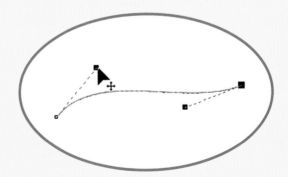

If you move the control points for a node, CorelDRAW plots a smooth curved path for the segment. By experimenting with the control points, you'll soon discover how to turn a straight line into curves and shapes.

Editing and controlling curves

Start with the most basic object possible – the straight line – and learn how to change it into any shape your drawing requires.

1 Start a new blank drawing in CorelDRAW. To add a straight line, first select the Freehand Tool and then click once on the page. Move your mouse across and click a second time.

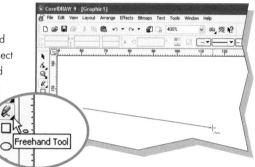

2 CorelDRAW adds the line to your page and places six handles around it. Look closely at the line itself and you'll see nodes at each end of the line – the larger one indicates that it is the original node.

3 To change your line's path, select the Shape Tool. The six handles then disappear, leaving just the two nodes. Right-click on the right-hand node and select To Curve from the pop-up menu. CorelDRAW adds two small squares, evenly spaced along the line.

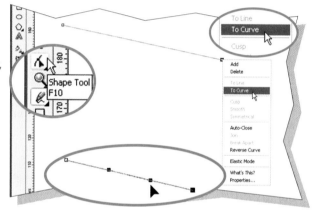

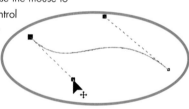

4 Notice how these squares are placed exactly on the line. This is a source of confusion to many CorelDRAW newcomers – these handles look like extra nodes on the line. In fact they are control points for the two nodes. Use the mouse to drag both control points slightly away from the line.

5 CorelDRAW does the Bezier maths to produce a smooth path for the curve. The exact path depends on where you place the control points. For example, the further away from its node that you place a control point, the more extreme is the deflection from the original straight line.

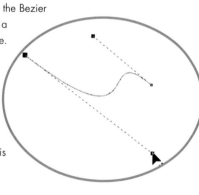

6 Although your line now has a more complex curved shape, it's still just a single segment. To add another segment, click either the second node or its control point and then on click the Add Node(s) button on CorelDRAW's Property Bar. An extra node appears on the line.

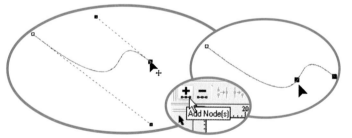

7 Click on this new node and you'll see that it has two control points instead of the single control point of the original nodes. This is because the line is now composed of two segments, joined at the central node. Try moving one of these new control points: notice that the other also moves – so as to keep the curve through the node smooth.

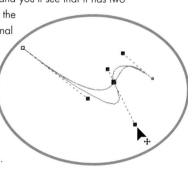

8 For additional control over the curve and to achieve sharper turns of the curve, select the node and click on the Make Node A Cusp button on the Property Bar. Now the node's two control points can be moved independently.

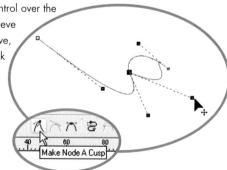

Drawing curves by hand

You can also draw shapes and curves directly on to your drawing and smooth out any unwanted wrinkles by editing the segments.

1 Start a new blank drawing and select the Freehand Tool. Draw an arch window shape by dragging the mouse with the left mouse button pressed. When the mouse returns to the first place you clicked and the pointer changes shape (top inset), release the mouse.

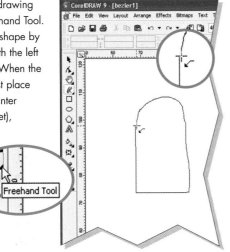

2 It doesn't matter how rough your outline is, because CorelDRAW automatically smoothes out most of the wrinkles. But it doesn't always guess right – and in this case has smoothed out our attempt at square corners.

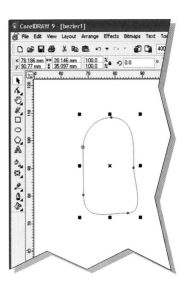

3 Now select the Shape Tool and move the two lowest nodes so that they are on the same vertical position on the page.

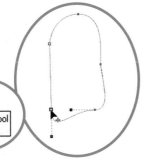

4 Next, select both of these nodes with the mouse. Click on the Convert Curve To Line button on the Property Bar. CorelDRAW straightens the line and removes any unnecessary control points.

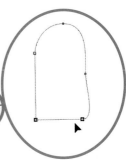

5 Repeat the process for the two side edges of the arch window. Then drag the two nodes at the base of the arch so they are directly above the lower nodes and also on the same vertical position on the page. Don't worry if the arch itself goes out of shape.

6 Now all that remains is to make the arch symmetrical. Start by clicking on the top node, then click on the Make Node Symmetrical button on the Property Bar. The control lines will now become the same length and the control handles move in unison. Move the node until it is placed exactly in the centre of the window and the control lines are level. Now, with this node still selected, look at the positions of the four control points, which dictate the path of the curve of these two segments.

7 Click on the node at the left side of the arch and move the control point until you have the arch shape you want. Then move the control points of the other side to match.

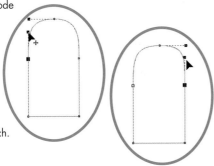

SHAPING YOUR CURVES

When CorelDRAW smoothes your freehand shape into a curved shape, it assigns one of three different types to each node: Cusp, Smooth or Symmetrical. Cusp allows sharp corners between segments, Smooth produces a gentle curve through the node while Symmetrical goes one step further and makes sure that the curve is the same on both sides of the node. You can change the type of a node by using the three buttons on the Property Bar.

Managing and layering complex images

You can make detailed pictures easier to handle by using layers to separate objects.

Images created in CorelDRAW are made up of numerous individual objects. The more complex the image, the greater the number of objects involved. This in itself isn't a problem, but moving and working with an image made up of a large number of objects can be awkward.

Moving objects is easier once they are grouped together, but this can then make it difficult to pick out a particular object for editing. To help manage this, CorelDRAW has a tool called Object Manager which opens a new window next to your drawing and displays the hierarchical structure of all the objects, showing you what is in front of what. One of the important ways that Object Manager helps is by allowing you to put objects into separate layers.

● Working in layers

Rather than attempting to work on all the different objects at any one time, you can assign related objects to their own layer. This makes it far easier to work on a particular aspect of the picture as you can grab hold of the individual components very quickly.

As a practical example, imagine that you created an architect's diagram, complete with plumbing and wiring plans. By layering the wiring details separately from the plumbing plans, you can work on one without disturbing the other – this also means that you won't accidentally alter the other.

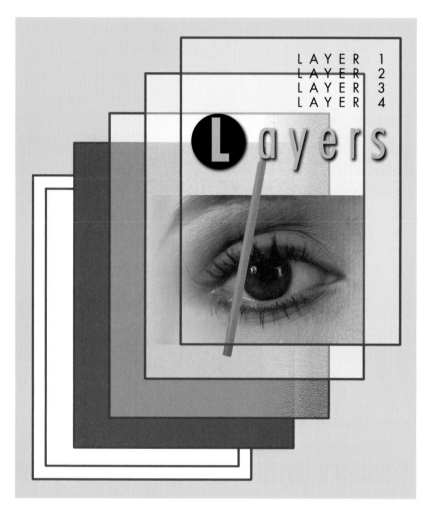

When a picture is split into layers, it's easier to move the component parts of the image.

You can also hide layers while you're not working on them. This can help a great deal by temporarily removing objects that might otherwise get in your way. It also allows you more space in which to work.

Another advantage of using layers is that you can make sweeping changes to all the objects within a layer simultaneously. For instance, you can select all layers in order to change the colours across the board, or swap layers between documents (allowing you to re-use a favourite background, for example, on other pictures). Once you get used to them, layers can make working on detailed pictures much easier.

WHAT IT MEANS

LAYERS

To help organize the component parts of a picture you can place various elements in a number of different layers. For example, the sun, clouds and sky in a landscape might comprise the background layer; some hills and a few distant trees another layer; a house another; and a person mowing the lawn, yet another. The overall effect is like grouping, except that you can move each component of a layer around independently.

● List editing

Even if you have assigned numerous layers, however, you might still have the problem of working with scores of little objects that make up the whole image. Object Manager allows you to select and edit an individual object by clicking on its listing rather than on the object itself. This means that you don't have to spend ages searching for the object you want to change, ungroup a grouped image, or try to keep your hand steady as you click on one of two objects a few millimetres apart.

Object Manager also comes in handy when cutting and pasting. It is much easier to deal with object names contained in the Object Manager list than to fiddle around with the actual objects themselves, and you also reduce the risk of accidentally moving or altering them instead of simply selecting them.

Object Manager lists a number of attributes for each object, so quite often you won't even have to look at the whole image to tell which object is which. A single icon indicates the type of object (curve, text, rectangle and so on) and its colour and thickness, while next to the icon a text description gives the style of its fill and the status of its outline.

Further uses for Object Manager include keeping account of additional pages if you are using more than one page when designing an image. These extra pages are displayed as

icons at the top of the list, and moving objects between pages is done in the same way as moving objects between layers.

● Master layer

If you are working with many pages, you can make use of the Master layer to help organize your work. This extra layer can be used to place the same information and objects on every page you are using.

For example, if you want some header or footer text, such as page numbers or chapter headings, to appear on each page of your document (see Stage 2, pages 44-45), you can instruct the Master layer to place the information on each page automatically.

Finally, Object Manager also works well with PowerClips. This powerful command allows you to place one object inside another. When the resultant image is viewed through Object Manager, the relationship between the two objects is far easier to see and, if necessary, to alter accordingly.

In fact, it's surprising how simple a complex image can become, and how easy it is to work on, when the component parts are listed in order in the Object Manager.

Introducing the Object Manager

Object Manager is at its most useful when you're working on complex illustrations, with hundreds of different elements, or a variety of layers. However, for this example, we're going to use a simple picture in order to demonstrate what Object Manager has to offer.

1 Load a piece of clip art from the CorelDRAW Essentials CD-ROM. We've used games069, which you'll find in the Track_fd folder, inside the Sports folder. From the Tools menu, choose Object Manager.

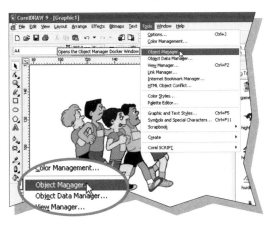

2 The work area will now have split into two parts, with your picture on the left and the Object Manager on the right. The Object Manager lists all the objects in the picture, along with text and icon descriptions of their style and shape.

3 If there's no group shown under the Page 1 icon, click on the small box with the cross (inset below) to expand the list.

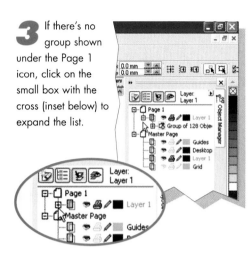

4 If you click on the picture in the work area, you'll see that the corresponding icon listing in Object Manager is highlighted. Click on the box next to the selected Group to see the full list of objects that make up the picture.

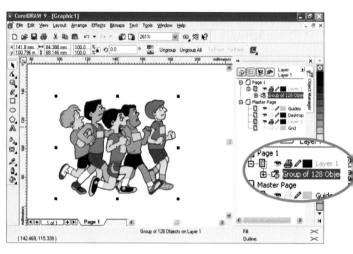

5 You can also select objects by clicking on their entry in the Object Manager list. Click on the box next to the icon for the Group of 128 Objects (inset). Then click on one of the Curves named C:0 M:16 Y:75 K:0 and the number card on one of the runners will be selected.

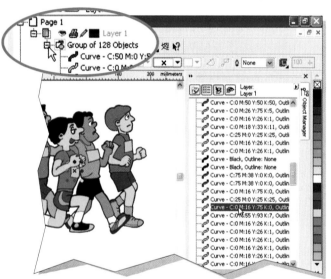

6 You can change the properties of objects using the Object Manager. We plan to change the orange number card on each athlete's vest to white. Click on each of the Curves named C:0 M:16 Y:75 K:0 in turn, making sure that a runner's number card is highlighted, and change the object colour by clicking on white in the palette running down the right side of the dialog box. The colour reference of the Curve will automatically change.

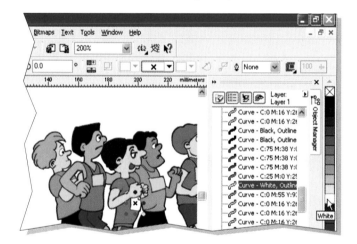

7 You can also delete items. Click on the third curve from the bottom and press the [Delete] key. The runner at the front loses his sandy coloured hair, and you see the black fill that's beneath it.

LAYER ICONS

Each layer name in Object Manager has three icons next to it. These icons are handy controls that help to organize and maintain the objects in their own layer. The eye icon represents whether the layer is visible on screen; the printer icon shows whether the layer will appear on a printout; and the pencil icon indicates whether the objects in the layer can be altered or edited. To change the status of a layer, the icons can be toggled (switched on or off) by clicking on them. When an icon is dimmed, that layer will either not be visible on screen, or not print out or not be editable.

Using these three icons allows you to concentrate your attention on specific areas of the screen. You can hide the clutter of other objects as you work, for instance, by toggling the eye icon so they are not visible. The printer icon allows you to add non-printing comments by putting them in a layer and toggling the printer icon so the comments do not actually print out.

Working with layers

Use the previous page's example to further transform the image.

1 At the moment all the objects are in the same layer, called Layer 1 in Object Manager. Rename the layer by right-clicking on it and choosing Rename. Call it something more meaningful – in our example we use 'Runners'.

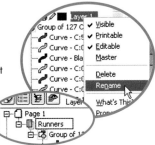

2 To create a new layer, click once on the New Layer button at the top of the Object Manager. Name it 'No5'.

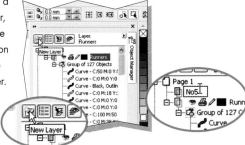

3 To move objects between layers, you drag them in the Object Manager. Before you can do this, however, you need to ungroup the runners. Click once on the picture in the drawing area and then click on Ungroup on the top menu bar.

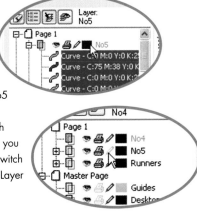

4 Each runner consists of lots of objects. If we are to make several or more complex changes it will be easier to re-group the objects by runner. Do this by dragging the pick tool over the first runner. All the objects belonging to that runner will be highlighted. But there are some objects which overlap from the runner behind him. Hold down the shift key and carefully de-select that runner's objects.

5 Now you can drag the first runner's group of objects in the Object Manager from the Runners layer to the No5 layer you just created. Continue doing this with each of the runners. As you separate each runner, switch off the pencil icon (see Layer icons box, opposite).

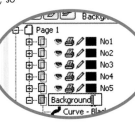

6 Using layers makes it easy to work with a particular part of the picture without disturbing others. There's no practical limit to the number of layers you can use or what you can use them for, so feel free to experiment. Here, we are just going to add numbers to the cards on the vests.

LAYER SAFETY

When working with multi-layered drawing objects, it is a good idea to save a copy in a safe place before doing any editing. If you make a mistake, you can always revert to your saved copy. Also, it can be useful to write down the main objects and layers in the image before editing begins. This will speed up your work and reduce the chance of mistakes being made.

7 To add text to the card, just highlight the area where you want to place the number, select the Text tool from the toolbox and give the runner an appropriate number. You will also see that a new object appears at the top of the layer in the Object Manager (inset below).

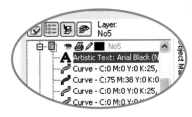

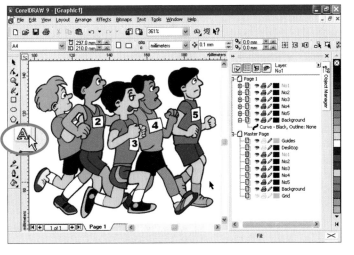

File formats and picture quality

Choosing to save your images in different formats can have a tremendous effect on the quality of the picture and the size of the final file.

The Corel suite of programs provides a number of alternative ways in which to save your images. Each offers a different file size and quality of image; which one you choose depends on how and where you are going to use the image you are saving.

Whenever you save a file, the information in that file is stored. The structure of the stored data is called the format and you choose this when saving the file by selecting the three-letter extension.

● Three little letters

All formats have a unique three-character extension, which is automatically added to the end of any file created in that format. In Word it is usually .DOC and in Excel it is .XLS, for example. The extension tells Windows (and any program that needs to open the file) the kind of information that will be in the file and how it is written.

File formats are relevant to all types of document, whether they have been created in a word processor, a spreadsheet or a graphics package. However, picture formats tend to be more varied and more complicated than most. There are a couple of reasons for this.

First, some graphics formats are better than others for storing the high-quality files used in colour magazines. These files can be very large (over 30MB) and the choice of format can make a big difference to file size. You may decide to use other graphics formats when it's more important to keep files very small. For example, the smaller the graphics used in Web pages, the faster they will download when you are browsing the Internet.

Some people choose to use certain formats purely because they are preferred by their graphics program. In Corel PHOTO-PAINT, the preferred format is CPT whereas Microsoft Paint prefers the BMP format. Typically, such formats allow you to use the widest possible range of features offered by the program but, as a result, they can end up being large and often can't be read by other programs. The CPT format of PHOTO-PAINT, for example, can rarely be opened by another program, which can be a problem if a file needs to be shared.

● Choosing a format

Fortunately, very few graphics programs are limited to saving files in their own unique formats; almost all allow you to use a number of common alternatives that enable you to swap pictures between programs.

It might not always be immediately obvious exactly what difference a particular file extension makes to the way an image finally appears. However, when comparing different file types 'under a microscope', the differences are more apparent.

It's important to distinguish between two fundamental types of picture: vector-based images, such as CDR files created in CorelDRAW, which are made up of lots of different drawn shapes; and photographic images, such as BMP files, which are made up of tiny pixels. To transfer vector-based files between applications, it's often necessary to convert the format into a pixel-based one – a process you can't reverse. Consequently, you might need to keep numerous copies of the same file in different formats to make editing easier.

In the panel below, we describe the most common alternatives, along with their advantages and disadvantages.

CorelDRAW ®

Different image types

PHOTO-PAINT can save images in a huge range of formats, each of which has its own particular uses. Here we describe the five most commonly used file formats.

WHAT IT MEANS

LOSSY

There are effectively two different types of compression. The first squeezes the file into a small space for storage and unsqueezes it when you want to work on it. Examples include WinZip or LZW compression. The second type strips the picture of fine detail, radically reducing its file size at the same time as compressing it. The stripped information is irrecoverable, which can cause a loss of quality and is described as being 'lossy'.

● BMP

BMP (Bitmapped) is a very popular file format as it is Windows' default format for pictures. It is often the file format for the Windows Desktop background, for example.

All graphics programs will be able to work with BMPs, but it is not possible to view them through Web browsers. Although they are unwieldy in their uncompressed state, BMP files do compress well.

● CPT

This is the default Corel PHOTO-PAINT file format. It is similar to the Windows BMP format, but includes additional PHOTO-PAINT information, such as printer settings and tool preferences.

This format is very useful when working exclusively in PHOTO-PAINT, but few paint programs recognize the file type. Therefore, you may have to save your file in an alternative format if you want to transfer it to another program or upload it to the Internet; keep the original as a master version.

● JPG

JPG is the most common image format on the Internet. The acronym is short for JPEG, which in turn stands for Joint Photographic Experts Group. The format is popular because it creates small-sized files while still being able to offer up to 16.7 million colours. This is ideal when you are using the Internet or when you are trying to squeeze as many pictures onto a floppy disk as possible.

When saving pictures in JPG format, you can choose the amount of lossy compression you want. If you choose a low setting, you can achieve quite good compression without the loss in picture quality becoming too noticeable. At high compression settings, the image becomes noticeably 'blocky'.

● GIF

Like JPG pictures, GIF (Graphics Interchange Format) pictures are viewable in Web browsers and because of the increasing popularity of the Internet the GIF format has become important for graphics users. However, it has one main weakness: where all the other graphics formats covered here can store photo-realistic pictures containing millions of colours, the GIF format stores a maximum of 256 colours.

When saving a picture in GIF format, the program simplifies the colours used. However, the file size of GIFs is very small indeed – and without being lossy either.

● TIF

The TIF (Tagged Image File) format is very popular among professional graphics users. Most graphics programs allow you to save in this format. It can store images with millions of colours, and includes LZW compression (see below), which provides a means of reducing file sizes without any reduction in image quality. TIFs, however, can be rather large, even when compressed.

LZW COMPRESSION

One of the highest quality compression techniques was invented in 1977 by Jacob Ziv and Abraham Lempel, two mathematicians. It was later refined in 1984 by Terry Welch. Therefore, LZW stands for Lempel-Ziv-Welch. LZW compression can be used on both text and image files and works by detecting repetitive sequences of information in the original file. For example, if you save a text file with the word 'the' in it 42 times, then LZW only stores 'the' once. It notes that the other instances of it are identical to the first, thereby removing the need to save the same piece of data in 42 places.

How formats affect quality

Save a colour image in different formats using PHOTO-PAINT.

1 Start with a bright image that contains lots of contrasting colours. We've chosen a photograph of fruit, which shows many different hues and shades.

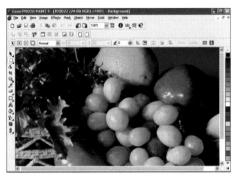

2 We'll want to try some format changes, but first you must save the picture as a CPT file so that you can come back to the original image for comparison.

3 To save the image in GIF format, first convert it into a 256-colour picture: click on the Image menu, then the Mode option and then select the Paletted (8-bit) option.

4 PHOTO-PAINT lets you choose the type of palette; select Optimized from the drop-down Palette box. PHOTO-PAINT now analyses all the colours in the picture and chooses 256 that can best represent the colours in the original. A preview image will appear on the right of the screen. At first it doesn't look too bad. Click on OK.

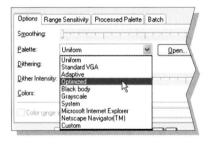

5 When the conversion process is complete, you'll see the image flicker and change. As you can see from our before (left) and after (right) examples, the effect is noticeable.

6 Select Save As from the File menu and in the Files of type box choose GIF – CompuServe Bitmap from the drop-down list of formats. PHOTO-PAINT automatically changes the file extension to .gif. (If you can't see the file extension, see PC Tips, below right). Save the picture into the same folder as the original. Click on OK in the dialog box (right).

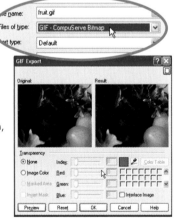

7 Now open the original CPT file again and select Save As from the File menu. This time when the dialog box appears, select JPG – JPEG Bitmaps from the list of file formats. Click on the Save button.

8 PHOTO-PAINT lets you set the amount of compression: drag the Compression slider three-quarters of the way to the right. Click on OK.

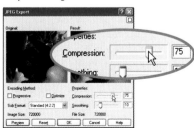

9 It doesn't look like the image has changed at all, but this is due to a peculiarity in the way that PHOTO-PAINT works. Close the image and open it again (make sure to open the JPG version you just saved). You'll now see that the lossy compression has caused small blocks to appear in the image.

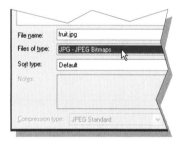

PC TIPS

Showing file extensions

Although picture file formats are related to a particular file extension, Windows XP hides the three-letter extension from view on many PCs. If the extension in the Save As dialog box (Steps 6 and 7) isn't visible, select Control Panel from the Start menu. Double-click the Folder Options icon and scroll down the list of settings. Untick the Hide extensions for known file types option and click on the OK button.

How formats affect file size

We'll now try some of the other file formats. Although these don't affect the quality of the image, they can have a marked impact on the size of your files.

1 Open the original CPT file you created on page 80 and, without changing anything, choose Save As from the File menu. This time, select the TIF – TIFF Bitmap format; as you do, you'll notice that the Compression type box changes, allowing you to choose from two options. Make sure that the Uncompressed option is selected and click on the Save button. Note: you won't see any change in the picture, because the TIF format is not lossy.

2 Now save the picture as a TIF again, but select the LZW Compression option from the Compression type box. Give it a slightly different name (we've chosen fruitlzw.tif), so that it doesn't overwrite the TIF you saved in Step 1.

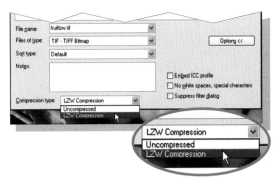

3 Save the file yet again, but this time select the BMP – Windows Bitmap file format (there are no compression options for this format) before you click on the Save button.

4 Close the PHOTO-PAINT window and open the folder that contains the files you have saved in these exercises. You can see your picture files listed. We want to see the sizes of the files, so select the Details command from the View menu.

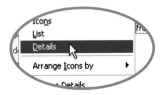

5 You can now see the files listed, with one file per row. Click on the Size column heading button twice and the list will be sorted in descending order of size. You can see that at the top is the uncompressed TIF file, with the BMP file fractionally smaller. Then comes the original CPT file and the LZW compressed TIF, around 30 per cent smaller. Then come the lossy files: first the GIF, which is around a quarter of the size of the CPT file. Much smaller, however, is the JPG file – around one tenth the size of the GIF and a massive 96 per cent reduction in file size from the original CPT file.

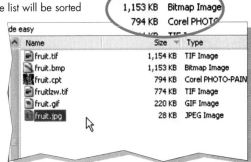

Which type of compression?

As you can see from the exercise above, the smallest file sizes are created by the lossy or 256-colour file formats. These GIF and JPG files are most useful if you're creating pictures for your Web site (see Stage 3, pages 132–135). The question is, which is better? For photographic pictures, the JPG format will provide better images. The colour loss isn't quite so obvious and with lower compression settings – between 10 and 50 – you'll still get reasonable image quality. Repeat Steps 7, 8 and 9 on page 80 with different settings to get a feel for how far to push the compression before it gets too obvious.

However, for some types of picture, the JPG format creates ugly and distracting effects and the GIF format may well prove more useful. For example, the simple four-colour logo (left) has a noticeable distortion along the edges when saved using the JPG format (inset).

When the same picture is saved in GIF format, there is no distortion at all; the limited number of colours in the original image ensures that there's no loss of quality when it is converted to 256 colours.

In general, where the original image has lots of subtle tones and shadows blending into each other, the JPG format works well, but where the image is made up of solid and continuous areas in a few colours, the GIF format is better.

Using Artistic Text

Special effects with text can be highly effective. Use your artistic judgement when experimenting with these effects and explore how you can attract more attention to your work.

CorelDRAW has a wide range of graphic options and special effects – and this is also the case when it comes to text. We've already seen how to use Artistic Text to create special characters (see Stage 3, pages 70–73) but you can also combine text with other objects to make even more effective designs. Here, we show how to exploit Artistic Text and turn a few words into an effective logo.

Artistic Text is most useful for applications such as logos or headlines, where you just want to add a single line or two of text. Once the words are placed on the screen, you can then add any of the standard CorelDRAW effects to create unusual and unique styles, which have great impact. Large blocks of text containing several sentences are best entered using Paragraph Text instead (see pages 84–85). Typically, such text needs only simple formatting – bold, italics, and so on – rather than special effects.

● Click here to begin
Artistic Text is created by selecting the Text Tool and single-clicking anywhere on the CorelDRAW page. A flashing cursor will then appear on the page, indicating that you can

begin typing. As we have already seen, the main benefit of Artistic Text is that text is treated like a series of drawn objects that can be manipulated, rather than simply edited as you would with a word processor.

You have the choice of tweaking individual letters or adding overall effects to whole words. You can choose any of CorelDRAW's standard graphic effects but most often you'll probably want to add a special type of fill to the text or to give it some depth and an illusion of 3D modelling.

● For my next trick...
Another very useful ability of Artistic Text is that you can use it to fit text into a shaped area. By simply clicking on the edge of an object, you can make the text to run around its outline as you type. This effect can be further refined so that the text appears to run around the inside of the object or at a specified distance away from it. You can even make the object invisible after you have typed the text so that the text itself looks as if it is defining a shape.

We touch on all these aspects of Artistic Text in the following exercise, in which we create a logo for a local football team's badge.

WHAT IT MEANS

PARAGRAPH TEXT
Paragraph Text is the alternative to Artistic Text. It is also created using the Text Tool but, instead of just clicking on the page to type in your text, you must drag a rectangular text box for the Paragraph Text to appear inside. Once this is done, it behaves much like a word processor and you can use standard word-processing commands to set aspects such as line spacing, alignment and simple text formatting.

Creating a badge with Artistic Text

In this exercise we'll be using Artistic Text to jazz up a badge design for the local football team. You'll see how text can be made to follow a shaped path and how you can apply any of the standard CorelDRAW effects to liven it up.

1 First we need to create a badge with a picture on it. We'll do this using an ordinary circle and a piece of clip art of a football. Draw the circle using the Ellipse Tool, holding down the [Ctrl] key to make sure a perfect circle is created. Fill in the circle with a solid colour.

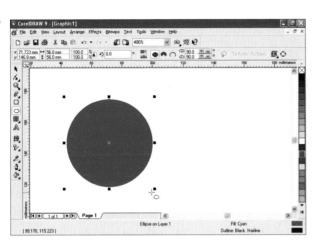

2 Now import a football from the CorelDRAW clip-art CD-ROM (see Stage 2, page 75). We've used Sball123.cdr from the Sports/Soccer folder. You might have to shrink it from its original size to fit the badge.

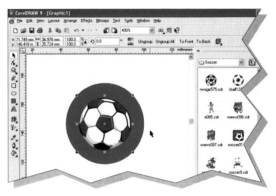

3 Running text around a path works only with simple objects, rather than grouped ones like the football clip art. To get around this problem, draw an unfilled circle around the football as a guide for the text. We'll make the circle invisible later.

4 Now choose the Text Tool from the toolbar on the left. Move the cursor onto the edge of the new circle and you will see the cursor change to a small 'A' over a curved line (right).

Click on the left mouse button and type in your text. You'll find that it follows a path running round the outside of the circle around the football (above).

5 You can change the way the text follows the path by using the drop-down list boxes on the Property Bar. For example, try changing the Distance from Path setting to move the text away from the circle outline.

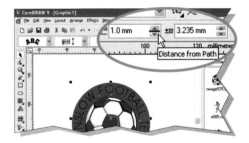

6 Now hide the guide circle. Right-click on the outline and choose Properties from the pop-up menu (inset). Choose the Outline tab of the Object Properties dialog box (below) and click on the button in the top right-hand corner. Click on the Apply button to turn off the outline.

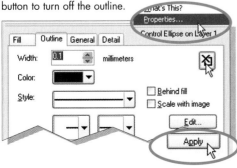

7 The circle will disappear, leaving the text in place.

8 To finish off, you can insert some more Artistic Text at the bottom of the badge and then add a special effect. From the Effects menu, choose Add Perspective and pull the two bottom corners of the text box outwards, to give a distorted effect to your text.

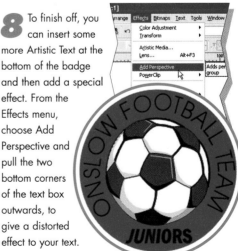

Flowing text

Here we show how the Paragraph Text commands can make your documents more eye-catching by running the text around pictures and shapes.

We've seen how text can be fitted around shapes using Artistic Text (see pages 82–83). You can also convert text into curves and distort the letters into fun shapes (See Stage 2, pages 73–74). However, these processes have a drawback: once converted, you can no longer deal with the words as text. This means that if, for example, you notice a spelling error after conversion, you can't amend it. You might even have to start again from scratch.

Paragraph Text, on the other hand, lets you manipulate the shape of a block of text, while still allowing you to edit and format it in the usual way – with bold, italics and different typefaces, for instance. If you want to make text a bit more interesting, you can also make the formatted text flow around, inside and between objects, creating eye-catching designs in the process.

● Wrapping blocks of text

You can make text run around either the outside or the inside of an object. To run text around an object, you simply apply the Wrap paragraph text command. This works for an object of any shape, including those you have drawn yourself. To confine text inside an object, you can adjust the Envelope of the object (see Stage 3, pages 70–73). You have the choice of a number of preset envelopes, or you can draw your own – both are easily editable. Alternatively, you can fit text within an existing object by clicking the Text Tool on an object and entering the text when the pointer changes to a box with 'AB' inside.

When wrapping text around irregular objects (such as the runner shown opposite),

PARAGRAPH OR ARTISTIC?

Although both are created using the same tool, there is a significant difference between Artistic Text and Paragraph Text. Artistic Text is used for single words and short sentences – the letters themselves are treated as individual objects – while Paragraph Text is used for longer strings of text. As a general rule, text that is more than one sentence long is best entered into CorelDRAW as Paragraph Text, and any short phrases or titles as Artistic Text.

there are two approaches. CorelDRAW normally wraps text so that it follows the object's outline. However, for some irregular shapes this can make the text harder to read, as it wraps around every nook and cranny. In such cases, you should add a regular shape – such as a circle or a rectangle – for the text to wrap around. You can then hide the shape by removing its outline so that it is transparent.

Flowing text into a poster

Here we create a poster for a school sports day, featuring a picture of a runner with words wrapping around him.

1 First, we want a central object to be the basis of the document. The text for our poster will come later. Draw your own central object, or insert some clip art. Here we've used pekc043j – from Sports/Track_fd on the CorelDRAW CD-ROM.

2 Although paragraph text will flow around an object of any shape, it usually looks better with a uniform outline. Draw a circle around the runner and then make its outline invisible. Do this by right-clicking on the circle and selecting Properties from the menu. Then click on the Remove Outline button in the top right-hand corner under the Outline tab and click on Apply.

3 Next click on the General tab of the dialog box. Then tick the Wrap paragraph text check box. Click on Apply again.

4 We now need to add some text. Select the Text Tool and, holding down the left mouse button, draw a text box that covers the circle with at least a centimetre to spare on all sides. Type in the words – you can always copy and paste if you run out of inspiration. We have made the text a light grey colour and used a fairly small font size to make sure it doesn't overshadow the picture.

PC TIPS

Text offset

More often than not when adding flowing text effects, you will want to make sure that the text itself is not too close to the object; both the text and the object have more impact if they are clearly separated. You can easily change the amount of space between flowing text and the shape it is next to. Use the shape's Object Properties dialog box (see Step 2), choose the General tab and increase the value in the Text wrap offset box (below).

CorelDRAW ®

5 This looks reasonably good, but we can improve it by changing the shape of the text box. Select the Paragraph Text box and then choose the Interactive Envelope Tool. You can now move each of the box's handles to a new position. Click on the Property Bar's Add Preset button and then on the diamond shape.

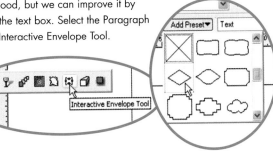

6 The text box changes shape, and the text inside it reflows to follow its new shape. Make the diamond shape fill the full height and width of the page by dragging its four handles.

7 Finally, create a series of triangles in each of the poster's corners and fit text into them. To draw a triangle use the Bezier Tool to define the three corners of the object. When you've finished, fill in each of the triangles with a bright colour.

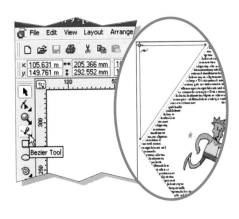

8 Select the Text Tool. Click on the edge of a triangle when the cursor becomes a box with the letters 'AB' in it. Type in the text so that it appears only in the triangle. Repeat with all four triangles to produce the finished poster.

Getting fast results with Artistic Media

CorelDRAW's powerful Artistic Media features make complicated artistic techniques a matter of simply clicking or dragging to apply them to your pictures.

With constant development for almost 10 years, CorelDRAW has added more instant art techniques with each new version. The idea is to make computer art so easy that anyone who can use a mouse can get quick art results.

If you're finding that CorelDRAW's standard collection of square, circle and line shapes isn't inspiring, try the Artistic Media effects. This collection of strokes combines shapes and special effects to create fantastic results – all in a few seconds.

● Pen mightier than the mouse

One of the most useful tricks that you can achieve with the Artistic Media tool is to simulate calligraphy with the mouse. The nib on a real pen draws lines of different widths depending on the direction of its travel: horizontal lines are thinner than vertical lines, for example.

With CorelDRAW, you can make your mouse emulate this effect if you choose the right Artistic Media option. This is great for creating simple Web graphics where you want to produce a hand-drawn effect. If you have a pressure-sensitive drawing tablet you can achieve interactive control over the thickness of the strokes. By pressing harder with the stylus on the tablet, you draw thicker lines in your drawing.

● Using images as strokes

Even without a drawing tablet, you can create 'hand-written' text in a variety of calligraphic styles. You can also use the typefaces installed on your computer as the basis for stroke effects. This is perfect if you want to jazz up some text on a poster or leaflet, but none of the typefaces on your computer is suitable.

Strokes aren't merely for jazzing up text – they work just as well with any type of line in your drawing. In fact, they can give a new lease of life to the simple rectangle, ellipse and polygon tools in CorelDRAW's toolbox. Often, when you know the basic shape you want but you're stuck for ideas about how to make it interesting, one of the ready-made strokes will suggest an approach that you wouldn't otherwise have considered.

CorelDRAW's strokes are very versatile. At their simplest, they're just black and white curved shapes which you can apply to another line. This results in a new shape that has the basic outline of the stroke but has been stretched and distorted to run from the start of the original line to the end of the line. As CorelDRAW treats all shapes as lines, you can apply these strokes to circles and polygons.

Personalize your documents by using the art tools CorelDRAW makes available to you.

For more drastic changes, there's a wide selection of coloured strokes, ranging from abstract patterns and rainbow effects, through to arrangements of leaves and animals. By applying these designs or image strokes, you can completely change the look of your original line or shape. Your original line is hidden from view by CorelDRAW, so it's impossible for people to see how easily you achieved the dramatic effects.

● Fast results and instant ideas

CorelDRAW's Artistic Media strokes allow you to achieve results way out of proportion to the time you put into using them. Once you have the hang of how they work, they're a powerful adjunct to CorelDRAW's regular drawing tools. Even if you just want to dabble, they're a great source of inspiration.

DIY STROKES

CorelDRAW's ready-made strokes are .CMX files and they are shown in the Artistic Media docker (display panel). The program lets you save any part of your own drawings as a .CMX file, so you can make strokes of your own. In the Files of type box in the Save Drawing dialog box select the 'CMX – Corel Presentation Exchange' option. By using the Browse button on the Artistic Media docker, you can also select your own strokes.

Artistic Media basics

It doesn't take much experimentation to learn the ins and outs of the Artistic Media commands – and the results are really worth while.

THE BASIC idea behind Artistic Media strokes is to apply a ready-made shape, image or set of images to a line. This line can be the outline of a shape in your drawing or a curved or straight line that you draw on the page. Many of the strokes can completely change the look of the line – often in ways that seem difficult to predict – so it pays to experiment a little before using these techniques in your drawings.

1 Open up a new CorelDRAW document. Select Artistic Media from the Effects menu to see the strokes available in the bottom part of the docker (the display panel, shown right and inset below).

2 Use the Freehand Tool to draw a straight line on a blank page. While it's still selected, double-click one of the strokes in the docker and CorelDRAW immediately applies the stroke to the line you have drawn.

3 If you do the same with a curved line, CorelDRAW applies the stroke along the path of the curve. Try this with several of the other ready-made strokes to see how they work. The effects are frequently amazing although they take very little effort to create.

4 Some strokes use your lines only as a rough basis for their position. Scroll down the list to see Object Sprayer strokes. These work like PHOTO-PAINT's Image Sprayer tool: several objects are sprinkled around the path of your line. You can also create a different picture using your original straight line and the same stroke by altering the Choice of spray order on the Property Bar to Randomly, Sequentially or By Direction.

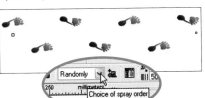

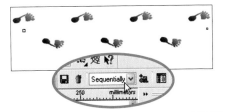

Drawing your own letters

CorelDRAW brings the power of the pen to your mouse by adding hand-drawn calligraphic effects to your lettering.

1 When you start CorelDRAW, the Artistic Media Tool is normally hidden from view. Click on the Freehand Tool in the toolbox to see the full range of line drawing options and select the Artistic Media Tool from the pop-up options.

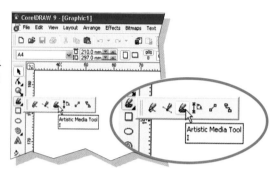

2 The Property Bar changes to show the relevant settings and options for this tool. To imitate hand-written text, first click on the Calligraphic button.

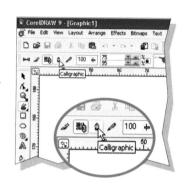

3 The mouse pointer changes to a pen shape when it's over the drawing area. Draw a letter shape to see how the tool works. You can create joined-up writing – as you'd write on paper – but it's best to start by creating a letter with distinct strokes, like the three strokes in this 'H'. Note that the vertical strokes in this letter are very thick, but the not-quite-horizontal centre stroke varies in thickness from left to right.

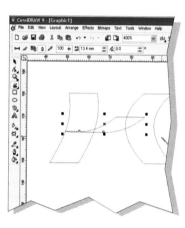

4 To apply solid colour to the strokes to see the letter more clearly, click on the black square in the colour palette. Although the letter looks like a solid shape, your three lines are still underneath. Drag one of the strokes to the side and CorelDRAW moves the one you originally drew.

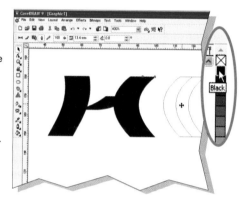

5 This makes it very easy to redraw the letter with different calligraphic settings. Select one of your strokes and reduce the figure in the Artistic Media Tool Width box on the Property Bar.

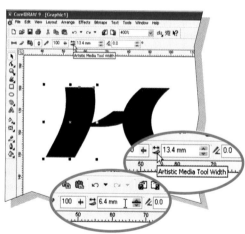

6 When you press the [Enter] key, the line is redrawn with the new setting. Repeat the same process for each of the strokes in your letter. In this version, the vertical strokes are no longer so dominant.

7 Experiment until you have a stroke thickness you're happy with, and then write the rest of the letters for your text in the same way.

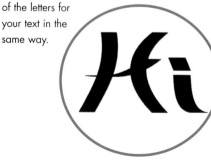

8 There's no end to the variations you can get. You can try different angles for the calligraphic nib – even after you've written your text. Just select all the strokes and type a new angle into the Calligraphic Angle box on the Property Bar (inset). Press [Enter] and CorelDRAW adjusts all the strokes accordingly.

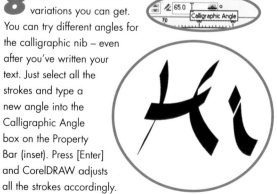

PC TIPS

Smooth lettering

If you want to write an 'i' or 'j', you might find it awkward to make the shape and place the dot in alignment over the downstroke. They can, however, be drawn with one stroke. The letter is drawn as a single stroke and a small rectangle is drawn to intersect it near the top. The rectangle is then changed to match the page's background colour.

Changing shapes into strokes

If you are looking for inspiration, use Artistic Media effects to turn CorelDRAW's standard shapes into something completely different.

1 We have adapted a business card taken from CorelDRAW's Business Card Templates. All it needs now is a finishing touch – something to represent the nature of the business.

2 There's plenty of gardening and plant clip art to choose from, but if used too often, clip art loses its impact. Instead, draw a circle on the blank area of the card and then select Artistic Media from the Effects menu.

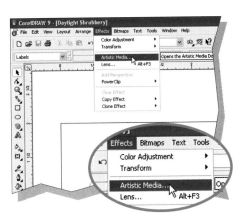

3 The Artistic Media docker opens on the right of the window. Select the circle, scroll down the list of Strokes and click on the a1.cmx stroke.

4 The original single circle outline is redrawn with a pinky-red stroke running clockwise from the top. It is thick to start with but thins out as it goes around the circle.

5 There are three shades in the stroke. Click a dark green colour in the palette.

6 Draw another, smaller circle inside the first and repeat the process, choosing another shade of green. Note how the stroke's 'paint' is concentrated at the top right of the circle. This happens because CorelDRAW creates a circle as a curved line that starts at the top and runs clockwise back to the top – the a1.cmx stroke is wider at the start and narrower at the end.

7 As the circles get smaller you may want to decrease the width of the pattern. The stroke can be adjusted to suit your image by changing the Artistic Media Tool Width setting.

8 Repeat the process for more circles in other shades. Eventually, with just a few circles, you have a smart-looking abstract design that would have been hard to achieve using the regular drawing tools.

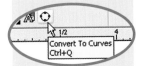

Manually tracing images

If you want to draw a realistic representation of an object or scene, tracing a photograph will save you time and effort.

Not everyone has natural artistic talent, and sitting down at a blank canvas to paint or draw is a daunting task for any novice artist. The same applies to computer art, but at least you can start off by using clip art to get a head-start, and any mistakes are easily reversed with the Undo command. Another way to get good results in CorelDRAW is to use a photograph as the basis for your drawing. By placing a scanned image or digital camera snapshot on a blank page, you will have a perfect guide from which to create your own drawing.

● Adding objects

Once you have added a photograph to the page, you can use any of the buttons on CorelDRAW's toolbox to add objects such as polygons, ellipses and straight and freehand lines. It's best to build up your drawing bit by bit. With the photo as your guide, you can be sure that the proportions are perfect.

One of the big plus-points of creating your drawing this way is that you can decide on the level of detail you want in the image. Some graphics programs have commands that automatically trace photos and turn them into drawings, but these often add too much detail. With manual tracing you can focus on the aspects you want and ignore irrelevant detail.

● Finishing your drawing

Once you're happy with your drawing, you can then use CorelDRAW's colour palette to match the tones and shades in the photo, or alternatively you can opt for different colours

to achieve a new look. All of the CorelDRAW tools that you've already used are available to you – you can use fills to create smooth blends of one shade to another, or even add textures and other effects to achieve a more striking result.

Tracing a photograph can be a straightforward way to create your own, stylized picture.

BE CREATIVE

Even when you use a photo as the basis for your artwork, there's no need to slavishly copy the original image. You can often create far more striking designs by altering the shapes within the image or by using a completely different colour palette. You can then use your 'design' for your own stationery or cards.

Tracing a photograph

Take any photograph and you can create a beautifully drawn version within a few minutes – perfect for times when you need quick inspiration.

1 You can trace any photograph, but it's best to start with something without too much detail. With a blank page open in CorelDRAW, select Import from the File menu. Go to the My Documents folder, then My Pictures and then Sample Pictures. Double-click on the Blue hills file (all Windows XP PCs have this image).

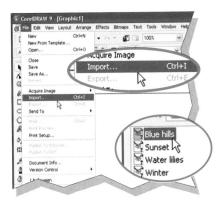

2 The mouse pointer shape indicates that it 'holds' the image. Click near the top left of the page. When the image appears, drag its bottom right corner so that it fills most of the page.

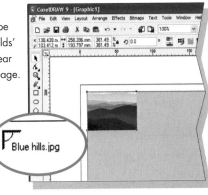

3 This image is composed of blocks of colour so we'll start by using the Rectangle Tool to add shapes that roughly correspond to the hills.

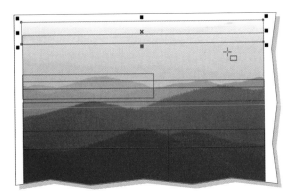

4 Now use the Convert to Curves command and the Shape Tool to alter the shape of these rectangles (see pages 70–73). Add nodes and modify the shapes to follow the hill outlines as accurately as you want for your final image.

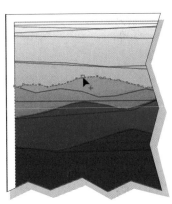

5 Once your shapes correspond to the image, you can start to add colour. Select each shape in turn and add a colour. Don't forget that the full range of CorelDRAW colour tools is available, including fill and texture.

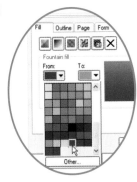

6 Once you have added colour, it's best to remove the outlines from the shapes. Use the Pick Tool to select all of the objects and right-click on the selection. Choose Properties from the pop-up menu and then use the No Outline button on the Outline tab to remove all outlines at once.

7 The result can be surprisingly effective. Within a few minutes you can often produce results that would take hours from scratch. Don't be afraid to simplify the image if it would improve the effect. In this example, we've used a single shape for the several blocks of colour in the original sky, and chosen a fill that accentuates the horizon.

PC TIPS

To avoid the possibility of inadvertently moving your underlying photo as you draw objects and tweak their shape, lock the photo to the page. To do this, right-click on the photo immediately after you have resized it and then select Lock Object from the pop-up menu. You can unlock it in the same way.

Saving graphics as PDFs

The Portable Document Format – or PDF – lets you publish your CorelDRAW files on the Web, while preserving the quality of your original file.

When you save the graphics you create in CorelDRAW Essentials, the program uses its own format – CDR – to store the information in the file. This format preserves the image perfectly. However, if you wanted to add this file to your Web site so that other people could see it you would come across a problem: not everyone has CorelDRAW on their PCs and, since very few other programs can read a CDR file, many people would be unable to open your file.

● From CDR to PDF

To tackle this problem, Corel enables you to save your graphic in Portable Document Format, or PDF. The PDF format was devised by Adobe specifically to help people publish files in a format that can be read by anyone on the Internet, regardless of the type of computer they have or the software they have bought. All you need is a small helper program called the Acrobat Reader (see Reading PDFs box, below).

When visitors to your Web site click on your PDF graphic, their Acrobat Reader program starts, interprets the PDF file and displays it in their Web browser. It's all handled behind the scenes automatically and means that you don't need to open files manually.

● Inside the PDF

One of the main reasons that graphics professionals use PDFs is that it preserves much of the quality of the original document, because of the way it saves text and graphics. It's possible to save your graphics in other

Web-friendly formats – such as GIFs or JPGs (see page 79) – but they are far from ideal for drawings or layouts that combine text and graphics. For example, they produce jagged edges on text if the visitor zooms in for a closer look.

When you save your graphic as a PDF, however, CorelDRAW presents you with options so that you can control the document quality to suit your needs. You can choose settings that optimize quality, or tweak them to end up with a file that's faster to download (see opposite).

Saving your file as a PDF means that you can be confident your work will be seen just as you intended it.

READING PDFS

PDFs are becoming a popular way of adding documents to a Web site for all sorts of Internet users, and many people have downloaded the Acrobat Reader program so that they can read PDFs. If you don't yet have it, visit www.adobe.com and you can download Acrobat Reader for free.

Publishing PDFs for the Web

Convert your CorelDRAW layouts into Portable Document Format files so that anyone can read them directly from your Web site.

1 Open one of the CorelDRAW layouts that you want to add to your Web site. In this example, we've used a map that combines graphics, directions and some descriptive text. Click on the File menu and select Publish To PDF from the menu.

2 This brings up the Publish To PDF dialog box. The first setting on the General tab covers the name and location for the PDF. CorelDRAW's suggestion is to use the same file name with the extension 'pdf', storing it in your My Documents folder. Click on the Browse button if you want to choose another name or location.

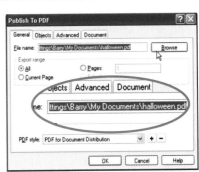

3 For multi-page documents, you can use the Export range settings to choose which pages to save; for our one-page document just ignore this setting. At the bottom of the General tab, select the PDF for the Web option from the PDF style box.

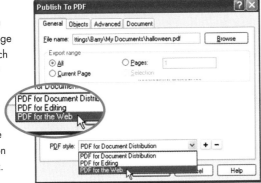

4 Now click on the Objects tab of the dialog box. These settings let you fine-tune the way that CorelDRAW compresses the text and graphics in your layout. If it contains bitmaps – digital photos or paintings you've created with Corel PHOTO-PAINT, for example – moving the Quality factor slider to the right will reduce the file size making the file quicker to download.

5 In the Text and fonts section, there are several useful options. For example, if you tick the Embed fonts in document option, CorelDRAW includes the fonts you have used. This way you can be absolutely sure that people viewing your PDF across the Internet see the text exactly as you designed it – even if they don't have the same fonts installed on their computer.

6 When you want to save the PDF, click on the OK button. CorelDRAW starts the conversion process. For long or complex layouts this may take a few moments, but one-page documents are converted very quickly, and the PDF file appears in the hard disk location specified in Step 2.

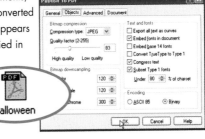

7 To check the file, double-click on its icon to open it in Adobe Acrobat Reader. You can now upload this file to your Web site.

PC TIPS

Some visitors to your site might not have the Acrobat Reader helper program required to read PDF files. It's good Net etiquette to let them know what they need and to include a link to the Adobe site so that they can download it and then come back and read your PDF files. There's no charge for adding a link in this way, and your visitors won't have to pay anything to download the program they need.

Hardware

The floppy disk

At well over 10 years of age, floppy disks are among the oldest computer accessories. Even today, however, they're very important, so it's useful to learn how they work, what they do and how to maintain them.

Ironically, today's so-called floppy disk is anything but flexible, but its name, derived from the days of the very early disks which were literally floppy, has stuck.

Like the hard disk inside your PC, floppy disks are a means of storing information. While they hold much less than a hard disk, they have the advantages of being small, cheap and easily portable. Typically, you can use them to store small files and documents so that you can move them easily from computer to computer and from office to home and back; they can also be used to back up your original files in case any are lost or accidentally deleted. While

'floppies' have been overtaken by newer technology, which can store many more and much bigger files, they're such a quick and simple storage medium that they're unlikely to become obsolete for quite a while.

● **Formatting your floppy**

Floppy disks work by recording the digital information of your files on to a thin disk of magnetic material divided into concentric 'tracks' and segments known as 'sectors'. Because the magnetic disk itself is highly sensitive, it is encased in a fabric liner and further protected by a plastic case. Before you can store any information on to floppy disks, you

may have to format them (see page 99). Some floppies are sold pre-formatted and can therefore be used immediately.

Modern floppy disks come in a standard size of 3½ inches wide and in two standard varieties of storage capacity: 720KB (or 0.72MB) and 1.44MB. These sizes refer to the capacity of the disk after you have formatted them, so don't be surprised if you see them sold as 1MB and 2MB floppy disks. A 1MB unformatted disk has a capacity of 720KB after formatting, while a 2MB floppy has

WHAT IT MEANS

FORMAT

A blank disk must be formatted before use. This process divides the disk into areas that your programs can use to store information. Think of these areas as a series of invisible circular 'lanes' on the disk's surface. The magnetic sensor in the floppy disk drive follows these lanes to write and read computer data.

a storage capacity of 1.44MB after formatting. A 1,000-word Microsoft Word file is about 15KB in size, so a 1.44MB floppy disk could store almost a hundred documents of a similar size.

You may also come across 2.88MB floppy disks. These were designed for use in special 2.88MB drives that were installed on only a very small number of PCs. However, this disk format did not really take off.

● Limitations of floppies

While floppies are ideal for copying or backing up smaller files and are eminently transportable and easy to swap between different machines, they are not able to deal with the size of modern software. A popular set of business programs, such as Microsoft Office, for example, can easily be

After using the floppy, eject it from the PC and store it carefully. Don't leave it next to an electrical appliance, as this can easily corrupt the data stored on the disk.

300MB in size, which would take up hundreds of standard floppy disks. Other programs are even larger. That's why almost all software companies now deliver their programs on CD-ROM discs, which hold up to 650MB of data.

Inside a floppy disk

Here's a visual guide to the parts that make up a standard floppy disk.

Protective cartridge
The plastic case is the main way of protecting the magnetic disk.

Write-protect tab and label
You can stop changes being made to the contents of the floppy by write-protecting, or 'locking', the disk.

Read/write slot
The slot through which your PC reads information from the magnetic disk.

Metal shutter
This slides back when you put the floppy into your PC.

Magnetic disk
This is where information is stored on the floppy.

Drive centre
Your PC uses this to spin the magnetic disk so that it can read the disk contents.

Fabric liner
An extra layer of protection for the material on the magnetic disk.

Checking space available on a floppy

Due to their limited storage capacity, it is always useful to know how much space you have left on your floppy disks. You can check this easily using Windows.

1 Insert the floppy disk in your disk drive, with the metal shutter end going in first and the label side facing upwards. Note that if you try to access the floppy disk drive when there isn't a disk present, an error message will appear, asking you to insert a disk into the relevant drive.

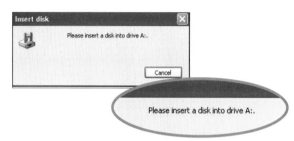

2 Select the My Computer entry from the Start menu to open the My Computer window. One of the icons in the window represents the floppy disk drive (A:). Move the pointer over this icon and select it with a single click. Now open the File menu and select Properties.

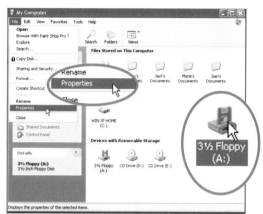

3 The screen that pops up will tell you how much space is left on your floppy, how much is used up and what the total capacity is. There is also a pie chart to help you see how full it is. The pink area is free space and the blue area is space occupied by your files.

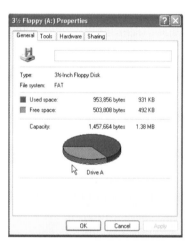

4 To show how this information changes according to the data you put on your floppy, copy a new file to it. Choose a file from your hard disk, say a Word or an Excel document, select Send To from the File menu, and then choose 3½ Floppy (A) from the sub-menu that appears.

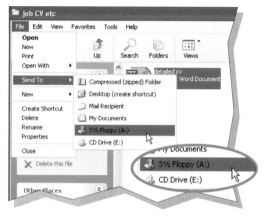

5 A window now pops up, telling you that the file you have chosen is being copied to the floppy disk in the A: drive.

6 When this is done, check the space on the disk again by selecting File, then Properties. You'll see that the blue area of the pie chart has increased, indicating that more space is occupied and the pink area has shrunk, showing that there is less free space.

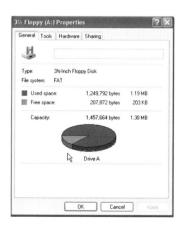

PC TIPS

Write-protected data

When trying to copy a file to a floppy, don't worry if you are told: 'Cannot copy [your file]: The disk is write-protected'. This means Windows has identified that the disk is protected from having files added or erased. It is called 'write-protect' because you can't write to the disk or take data off it, but you can read from it. You can choose whether or not to write-protect a disk by moving the small square tab on the corner of the disk to open the hole, often shown by a 'locked' symbol (inset). Make sure that a disk containing important data is write-protected.

Formatting a floppy disk

In order for a new floppy disk to work on your PC, it will need to be formatted. You may also want to format a disk that is full of old files. As formatting automatically wipes all data from a disk, this is often quicker and easier than deleting large numbers of individual files.

1 Insert a floppy into the disk drive. For this example, use one containing files you don't mind losing. Make sure the write-protect tab is closed (see PC Tips box, opposite). Open the My Computer window and click on the floppy disk drive icon.

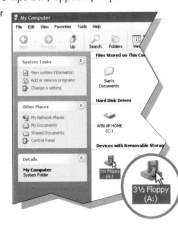

2 Go to the File menu and choose the Format option. You can also access the same option by right-clicking on the floppy disk icon and selecting from the menu that appears.

3 A new window opens, offering several options. The first of these is the capacity of your floppy. Choose 1.44MB or 720KB, according to the disk you are formatting. If you aren't sure of its size, select 1.44MB. If the disk turns out to be smaller, Windows will tell you and format it to the highest possible capacity.

4 You can give this floppy disk a short name by typing into the Volume label box in the centre of the dialog box. This name appears in the Properties window for the disk, helping you to keep track of your disks and data.

5 In the Format options section of the dialog box, the Quick Format box is not ticked by default. This forces Windows to do a low-level format – the type required when a floppy disk has never been formatted before. For this disk it's unnecessarily slow. Tick this box.

ALERT!

Be careful when formatting! Whether you choose a quick format or a full one, it will wipe all the data from your disk. You will not be able to retrieve any files lost in this way, so always write-protect a disk with important data on it. If in doubt, you can copy the floppy's contents to your hard disk until you are sure you no longer need the files.

6 When you've selected all the options you want, click on Start and Windows will begin to format your disk. As this will erase all your files, Windows asks for confirmation. Click on the OK button in the Format 3½ Floppy (A:) dialog box only if you're sure you don't need any of the files currently on the floppy disk.

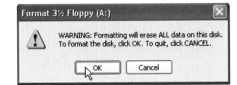

7 The floppy disk doesn't take long to format – especially if you ticked the Quick Format option. Click on the OK button when the Format Complete message appears.

Introducing DVD

DVD is the latest step in CD technology. It combines the functions of a CD-ROM, an audio CD and a video recorder in one disc.

The same size and shape as a normal CD-ROM, the Digital Versatile Disc (DVD) is the latest generation of CD technology. Utilizing both sides of the disc, a DVD can store up to 17 gigabytes (17,000MB) of digital information – this works out at about 26 times the storage capacity offered by a standard CD-ROM.

For the PC user, this means being able to get bigger and better Multimedia applications, massive reference works, games with video, sound and graphics (the likes of which haven't been experienced before) and, ultimately, recording systems offering almost unlimited storage.

With a picture quality three times better than that of a VHS tape, DVD also revolutionizes the way we watch movies at home. But this is only part of the story. DVD's phenomenal storage capacity allows movie studios to include alternative scenes or multiple storylines, letting the viewer choose which version of a film to watch.

Although each double-sided DVD disc is the size of an ordinary CD-ROM, it holds up to 17GB. That's around 26 times as much data.

A DVD drive looks identical to a conventional CD-ROM drive, and fits into the same space in your PC. It can read both DVDs and CDs.

The DVD's secret lies in its use of a blue laser to read information, as opposed to the red one found in a CD-ROM drive. The blue laser has a tighter beam and produces a smaller dot on the surface of the CD. This means that more dots (bits of data) can be placed on a DVD than on a conventional CD-ROM.

And, just in case you were worried, you don't even have to throw away your old audio CDs and CD-ROM collections. DVD drives can play audio CDs and computer CD-ROMs just as easily as the new DVD discs.

How to get DVD

You can enjoy the benefits of DVD today, either by buying a DVD computer or by upgrading your current computer. A computer with a DVD-ROM drive instead of a normal CD-ROM drive will not cost much more, as DVD-ROM drives have dropped dramatically in price. If your computer already has a CD-ROM drive, a dealer can replace it with a DVD-ROM drive for £50–£75 or you could choose to add an external DVD-ROM drive.

DVD-ROM drives connect to your computer and are primarily used for DVD software, although you can also use them to watch films. DVD players, however, connect directly to your TV – just like a video recorder – and can only be used to watch DVD films; DVD software will not work in them. It's also possible to connect DVD players to your hi-fi in order to receive a sound signal; if you have a compatible home audio system, you'll even be able to get surround sound.

The first of the few

Even though DVD has quickly become very popular, the format has not been without its teething troubles. The main problem is that film studios have used the introduction of DVD as a way of reinforcing international movie markets. So, while a Hollywood blockbuster will be released first in the US, it will only appear in Europe six months later. This is enforced in DVD through 'territory codes' (see Movies and territory codes box, right), which ensure that movies and software released in one area are not compatible with hardware sold in another territory.

Regions to be cheerful

For DVD users in Region 2 (the UK), territory codes can be a problem. They mean that if you purchase a DVD overseas, it might not work on your PC. However, some DVD drives can now overcome this problem with a special feature that lets you configure your drive for Region 1 or Region 2. There are often special settings, such as a switch on the unit or a button on the remote, that allow you to change between regions whenever you like rather than having to reconfigure the drive each time.

MOVIES AND TERRITORY CODES

For many years the big film studios have maintained a staggered release schedule across the world, launching a film in the US and then opening it in Europe around six months later. DVD allows the film studios to cement the boundaries between these markets in the following way.

The UK is in Region 2 – along with the rest of Europe, South Africa and Japan. This means that DVD discs bought in Japan will work on UK DVD systems, but the on-screen instructions might be in Japanese, even if the film has an English soundtrack.

America is Region 1 and it is illegal to sell US discs in the UK, although individuals are free to import them and play them on a US system or a DVD player that has been configured to Region 1.

Try visiting www.dvdreview.com to find out more about DVD news, developments and releases.

What DVD can do for you

Computers

A game that comes on four CD-ROMs, or a clip-art collection provided on 10 CD-ROMs, can be supplied on a single DVD disk. This format allows more gameplay and more sound, video and programs.

As they become increasingly affordable, DVD-RAM drives will offer home PC users almost unlimited removable storage.

Music

DVD-Audio provides better-than-CD sound quality, combined with multi-channel surround sound.

Movies

A DVD recorder that looks like an audio CD player will one day replace your VHS video recorder.

Although video currently has the edge on availability and price, the future belongs to DVD. This is due to DVD's impressive combination of features and the high quality of picture and sound. DVD also offers a number of additional features, such as the ability to go straight to a favourite scene, as well as extra scenes and Multimedia, and the provision of a choice of languages and commentaries by the director. Finally, DVDs are far easier to store than VHS videos.

Recordable DVD drives still cost more than £200, but as the technology develops and the market increases in size, you can expect the price to fall to less than £100.

Universal Serial Bus

Thanks to Universal Serial Buses (USBs), you can plug new hardware into your PC and use it right away without having to remember to install driver software or restart your computer.

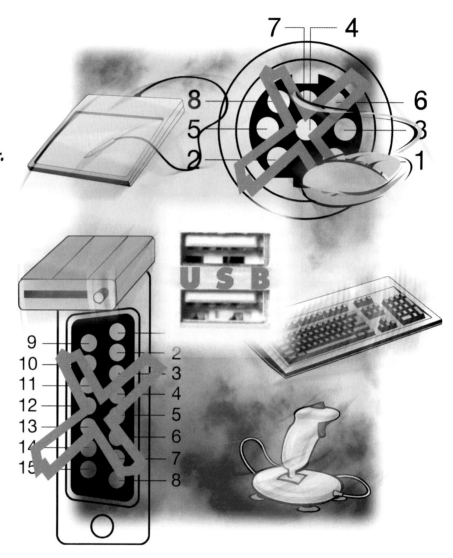

Behind almost every slick and fast PC is a real hotch-potch of sockets and ports. Initially developed to allow PCs to connect to specific devices – a printer or modem, for example – these many and varied sockets have outlived their usefulness. The Universal Serial Bus (USB) has changed all that: it's a way of connecting devices together and has become the standard for computers and associated hardware or peripherals.

● USB vs parallel and serial ports

The modern PC has many ports of different shapes and sizes: parallel, serial, a PS/2 socket for the keyboard and often another PS/2 port for the mouse. Usually, you simply plug a device into its own socket, but if all your ports are in use, you might have to unplug something you are currently using to connect a new device and then switch between the two.

To simplify matters, computer manufacturers adopted the USB standard, and now supply USB versions for almost every type of

external hardware. It features on printers, modems, joysticks, mice, keyboards, digital cameras, scanners, digital speakers, floppy and tape drives and many other devices.

● USB benefits

One of the greatest features of USB is that the devices don't each require a special port of their own on the back of the PC. This means

New PCs usually have a pair of USB sockets positioned on the back panel, but a few have an extra pair on the front panel – useful for quickly connecting or disconnecting devices such as digital cameras.

The Universal Serial Bus (USB) does away with a confusing and complex array of ports on your PC. USB sockets can accommodate all types of peripherals.

that you can plug a USB monitor into the USB port of the PC and then plug a modem, say, into the USB port of the monitor.

USB technology makes the day-to-day use of your PC more convenient, too. The USB port is robust enough to cope easily with the various new devices you might want to add to your computer, even while the system is up and running. You can plug and unplug devices as you please, without the hassle of having to restart your machine. The changes to your setup will be recognized immediately.

USB UPGRADE

If you have an older PC and so have no USB ports, do not despair. You can buy expansion cards that simply slot into your existing computer to provide the connection. In fact, you can opt for the latest type of USB ports – USB 2 – which are much faster than the USB ports fitted to most PCs. Expect to pay around £25 for a four-port USB 2 card.

All you have to do is just plug in this high-quality video camera from Logitech into a USB socket and it's ready to work immediately.

High-capacity port

The USB port is a modest-looking piece of equipment. One device, typically the monitor or the keyboard, plugs directly into the USB port on the back of the PC. This device can work as a hub, connecting the other devices to the PC. A maximum of 127 extra devices can be connected to one PC via USB, each one with up to 5m of cabling between them!

The inclusion of USB ports on a computer can be especially beneficial where two or more devices share the parallel port with conflicting demands as to which device has precedence, as in the case of an external Zip drive and a scanner.

In data transfer terms the USB port is a real flyer, dramatically reducing 'communication' time. This means that printers using a USB port should need significantly less time to print out your documents. The same applies to USB scanners, which also take less time to send the scanned information

GO-FASTER USB

The demands on PC hardware are always increasing and so, as good as the original USB specification was, it was unable to keep up with data-intensive connections like video cameras. For USB 2, the developers kept the same approach and the same plugs and sockets, but redesigned the chips to run at 40 times the speed. You can use USB 1 and USB 2 devices together, but to get the best performance you need USB 2 ports on your PC.

to the computer. In addition, the technology is fast enough to offer simple networking possibilities. For devices that need even more speed, USB 2 offers up to 40 times the speed (see Go-faster USB box, below).

Built-in power

Just as handy for the individual home computer user is the inclusion of a 5V power supply within the USB connector. This means that the USB cable can also supply the power to many USB add-ons so they no longer need their own mains adaptor. This

If you have a USB socket on your computer, think about replacing worn-out peripherals with USB-compatible ones, such as this mouse from Genius.

helps to minimize the number of cables that snake across and under your desktop. Also, printers, scanners and other USB devices can be placed further away from the computer itself, which helps to reduce clutter around your keyboard and screen.

There is no catch. USB applies the 'Plug and Play' principle (the ability to just plug the device in and start using it without restarting the PC) to external devices even more efficiently than it already works with internal devices. In the early days, there were a few teething problems with Plug and Play but these have been largely ironed out now, and the USB technology is extremely reliable.

USB and Windows

For USB to work, it requires the close collaboration of Windows itself. USB is intended to do away with the need for driver disks and set-up programs. Ultimately, all the necessary software will be built into Windows or

available for automatic download from the Internet. The idea is that it will be both loaded and unloaded automatically, as required. Until every PC has a fast connection to the Internet, however, new and innovative add-ons will still include a disk containing drivers. Even so, the installation procedures for both hardware and software are now much simpler than they used to be.

What has made the USB such a winner is the support it has gained from the computer 'giants'. Everyone who's anyone pushed it as a common standard: Microsoft, Intel, Compaq, IBM, NEC and Apple. With these companies behind it, and with new PCs now including the port as a matter of course, it really couldn't fail to be a success.

Where are USB devices?

USB peripherals of every kind are now available. In fact, if you bought your computer from 1997 onwards, it is likely that it will already have USB ports.

It's now only worth buying USB add-ons instead of the older, soon to be outdated, parallel or serial devices – even if they're slightly cheaper. That way, you'll have a head start as hardware in the future will definitely be based on the USB standard.

USES FOR USB

All manner of USB products are available. Much touted as a technology for Multimedia fans and gamers, USB already boasts a wide variety of joysticks and game controllers from all manufacturers. This is good news if you've ever struggled with the settings of a games device – possibly the most fiendishly tricky of all computer peripherals to install.

There are also USB digital speaker systems and digital cameras, and several monitor manufacturers have released a flat screen monitor that works as a USB hub. Of course, the simpler devices – mice and keyboards – are also available. In addition, if you opt for an ADSL connection to the Internet, the package will contain a USB ADSL modem to maximize the potential of the ADSL speed.

Message modems

All modems allow computers to talk to each other over telephone lines, but some also combine the capabilities of an answering machine and a hands-free speakerphone.

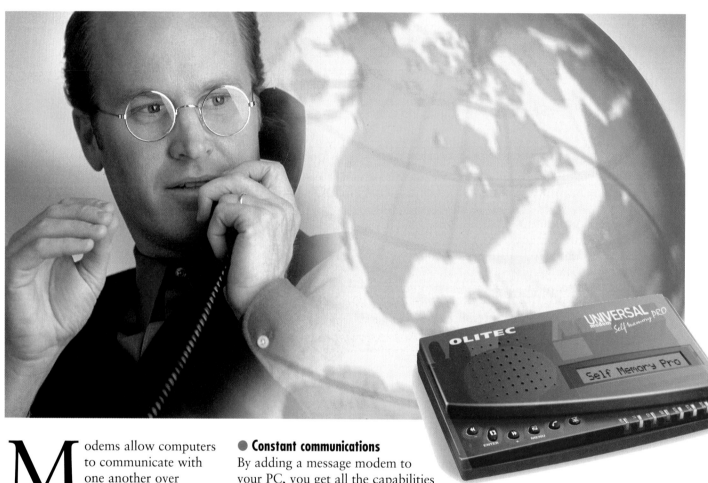

A modern modem, such as the Olitec Universal Self Memory Pro, can not only deal with your surfing and email but also answers the phone and takes messages.

Modems allow computers to communicate with one another over telephone lines – to swap emails or browse the World Wide Web, for example.

In addition to this, most modern modems can also act as fax machines, cutting out the tiresome steps of printing your fax, then having to wrestle with a separate fax machine to send it. Any faxes received can be displayed on the screen and then printed out, a factor which greatly increases your computer's potential as an all-round communications centre. Better still, a small number of modems are now able to deal with voice messages. Such models are called message modems.

● Constant communications
By adding a message modem to your PC, you get all the capabilities of a normal modem plus a built-in answering machine and fax store.

Some conventional modems come with special programs which give them similar capabilities, allowing storage of voice messages and faxes on the computer's hard disk. The problem with these modems is that the PC must be switched on the whole time so that the software can answer incoming phone calls and record them. This means the system is constantly consuming power and that you live with a non-stop hum from the computer's power supply.

A message modem, by contrast, has extra circuits and features that handle all incoming communications without needing to access your computer's hard disk to store the data. This means that the modem works whether or not your computer is switched on, although you will need to switch the computer back on to read faxes.

Of course, to be able to do its job while your computer is switched off, a message modem can't be dependent on the computer for its power supply. For this reason, you won't find any internal message modems. They are all external units, with their own power supply and their own control panel appearing on the casing.

The most important extra in a message modem is a large helping of computer memory. All modems have some memory, but it's usually only sufficient for storing a handful of settings. This extra memory is used for storing incoming voice and fax messages. The exact amount of information that a message modem can store depends on the amount of memory built in. Memory of 4MB, for example, gives enough space to store around 20 minutes of voice messages or up to 100 faxed pages.

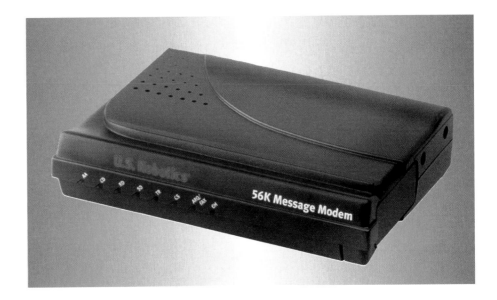

The US Robotics 56K Message Modem can replay your voice messages when you call in from any other telephone.

● How it works
To be able to store calls from people who telephone you, the message modem must first convert sound into computer data. Likewise, to replay the messages, the message modem must convert the stored data back into sound. You then hear this through the modem's built-in speaker.

Many message modems can also work as hands-free speakerphones. This means that you can use your PC to dial a telephone number and then all you need to do is ensure that you talk near the modem. A microphone built into the message modem picks up your voice and transmits it to the person at the other end of the phone line, while you hear that person's voice from the modem's speaker.

Message modems can be installed as easily as normal modems (see Stage 1, pages 140–141). The answerphone features are controlled by extra buttons on the modem itself. Faxes that have been received while the computer has been switched off can be viewed and printed once the computer is switched back on.

WHAT IT MEANS

FLASH MEMORY

All modems have a small amount of memory that contains tiny, but vitally important, software used to control the modem. In many modems this memory is permanent but some modems use 'flash memory' which can be overwritten, allowing you to upgrade the software from floppy disk or via the Internet.

Some modems offer extra voice features, but fall short of full message modem capability. For example, some use their built-in memory to hold email messages only. You can program these devices to contact your ISP and collect your email messages when your PC is switched off.

● Upgrading modem software
As with any modem, it's wise to buy with a view to the future. Many models are designed so that they can be upgraded by changing the modem control software. For example, some modem manufacturers have offered updates to make the modem work faster. Such upgradable modems are provided with flash memory and are less likely to go out of date.

In these cases, the modem manufacturer provides a program so that all you have to do to update the control software is run it on your PC. The program will then communicate with the modem and replace the old software stored in its flash memory chips with new software which can be downloaded either from the Web site of the manufacturer or direct-dial bulletin board.

Although the manufacturer's updates to the software can help improve your modem beyond its initial capabilities, they can only go so far. Unfortunately, it's impossible to keep upgrading to the newer standards so, while it can help for a time, don't expect even a flash memory modem to keep up with future changes indefinitely.

AUTO-ANSWER ALERT

While you might well want your modem to answer voice telephone calls automatically, you need to think through the consequences of letting your modem auto-answer calls from other computers. It can be a very bad idea. On the one hand, if you travel with a portable or notebook computer, being able to dial up and connect to a desktop computer at home to pick up files and information can, of course, be very useful. On the other hand, there is a risk: if someone else dials your telephone number, they might be able to gain access to your important files. Even home computer users need to be alert to this possibility.

To protect against this risk, you should read the manuals for your modem and also those for any communications software (such as fax programs) that you use. Programs that allow you to dial in and both see and use your computer's hard disk are known as remote access programs. If you need to use this type of software, check the manuals for the sections that deal with security aspects. Passwords, for instance, can make it much harder for someone to break into your PC, and extra layers of security – such as getting the modem to hang up and then dial you back – make it even tougher.

Videophones

With some easy-to-install technology, you can speak 'face-to-face' with people all over the world.

The notion of a device that allows you to see someone at the same time as you speak to them – the videophone – has been around for over 50 years. For a long time, however, it was firmly in the realm of science-fiction fantasy, but now it's a cheap and easy reality for anyone with a PC and an Internet connection. In fact, the hardware itself has become so cheap and so widespread that many PC makers will supply everything you need as part of a new system. Even if you are adding to your existing setup, your outlay will be well under £40.

● Who needs it?

Videoconferencing, as such hardware is known, has widespread and obvious advantages. In business, it can save time and money by allowing home-workers or colleagues and collaborators to communicate face-to-face without travelling. For large meetings, where many people might be present in the same room, highly sophisticated and expensive equipment is needed. But if you just need a one-to-one chat with the boss, then all you require is the kind of home hardware set-up we are looking at here – and it is principally in the home environment that cheap video-conferencing is really taking off.

WHAT IT MEANS

USB

The Universal Serial Bus (see pages 102–103) is a method of connecting computers and devices such as modems, mice and video cameras. It's fast and can link up to 127 devices in a daisy-chain arrangement. It is designed to improve upon – and eventually banish – the serial and parallel ports of today's computers. The best aspect of USB is that you do not have to turn off your computer when you want to attach or disconnect a USB device.

A videophone not only makes communication more fun, it also makes it much more likely that you will understand exactly what people are talking about.

● What you need

The basis of home video-conferencing software is the Web cam. These small cameras – some so tiny you can literally fit them in a shirt pocket – supply the video images you see on Web cam sites. On these sites, a camera is pointed towards an area of interest and you can log on at any time to see what's happening.

There is a wide range of Web cam manufacturers, including Logitech, Philips and Kodak. Some models resemble a large golf ball, while others have a squarer design. The camera will be supplied with some sort of base that allows you to position it in a convenient place – typically, on top of your monitor so that it is pointing straight at you while you work. Alternatively, it can be placed just about anywhere you want to capture the images that you wish to transmit.

The most popular way of connecting a camera to your PC is via the USB socket. You can also get Web cams which work with older PCs that lack USB sockets. The advantages of USB connections are that they are easy to use (you simply slot them in) and they do not take up a connection that you might need for another device, so you don't need to swap them around.

The other vital element of the package is the software supplied. What you get varies slightly from manufacturer to manufacturer. You will usually find some kind of video-conferencing software included, such as Microsoft NetMeeting, to allow you one-to-one connections with other users, and video-mail software which enables you to send moving images with sound via your email package. Even a simple graphics package – which allows you to improve still images before you send them – will often be included. In addition, the package might also install a number of popular audio and video plug-ins if it does not find them on your computer.

● Image quality

A Web camera will not produce particularly high resolution images; there is too much data to be

CHECKPOINT ✔

VIDEOPHONE ESSENTIALS

You'll need the following equipment and software to get the best from a camera:

☑ A Web cam with the right type of connection socket for your computer (make sure you check your computer before buying the camera).

☑ A computer with a spare port to accept the signal from the camera.

☑ A modem or broadband connection to the Internet.

☑ A microphone so that your callers can hear you.

☑ A sound card and speakers so that you can hear your callers.

☑ Software and drivers compatible with Windows XP.

transmitted so images are best displayed at a lower resolution, having been compressed by software. The drawback of this is that you lose some detail and the image will usually look jerky. To keep things manageable, the image size is relatively small compared to your screen area; around 15 per cent of the monitor's screen area is typical. Having said all this, for such cheap hardware the quality you get is surprisingly satisfying.

Sending emails with still-picture attachments or vmails (video mails) with moving images and sound are two of the most popular ways of using a Web camera. If you want to use it for video-conferencing or chat, then you have two possible methods of connection.

The first of these is by direct dial-up, where you call the number of another videophone user; their system must, of course, be set up and they must be

ready for your call. The second, which you might use if you want to chat to a variety of people, is to use an Internet connection to log on to a service such as CUseeMe (www.cuseemeworld.com) which enables real-time, face-to-face communication over the Internet. CUseeMe Web is available as a free downloadable plug-in.

VIDEO QUALITY

The quality of the video image transmitted by a Web cam over a conventional modem and telephone line is good, but is ultimately hampered by the telephone line. If you want better video quality, rather than a better Web cam, you need a faster connection. A broadband connection – such as ADSL – can give any Web cam a significant boost in video quality, but remember that to get the most out of it, both parties on the videophone need ADSL.

Installing and setting up a Web cam

Adding a Web cam to your PC is easy: just plug the camera's USB plug into a vacant USB socket on your PC and use the installation CD-ROM to set up the camera's software.

1 Connect your Web cam to one of your PC's USB sockets. Within a few moments, Windows detects the new hardware and the Found New Hardware Wizard window pops up. Insert the CD-ROM that came with the Web cam, ensure the top option is checked and then click on the Next button.

2 Windows checks the CD-ROM and locates the file that contains the driver software for your Web cam. It displays the camera name – in this case a generic Web cam. Click on the Next button and Windows copies the required files from the CD-ROM to your hard disk.

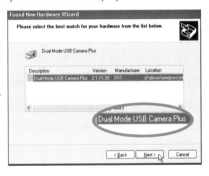

3 When the software installation is complete, start your Web cam program from the Start menu. Position the Web cam – most people prefer to place it on top of the monitor – and check the image in the Web cam video window.

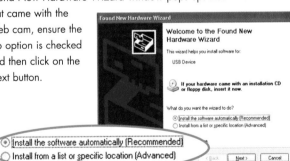

4 You may need to alter the Web cam software settings to get the best possible image. Look for a Settings or Camera Controls command within the menus. This will bring up a dialog box that provides several controls – usually in the form of sliders. Experiment with different settings and click on the OK button when you are happy with the image.

Label printers

If you find it tricky to print labels on your regular printer, take a look at label printers. These are custom built for the purpose. Using one might prevent you wasting both labels and time.

With a label printer you can print labels for everything from personalized stickers for private or business use (above) to your video tape collection (below).

Your computer is well equipped to print labels with Word. Despite this, label printing – especially in small quantities – can still be problematic. There are several reasons for this.

First, you need to remove the plain paper from your printer and replace it with special label pages. Second, you need to make sure your software knows how to use these labels. Finally, you may need several trial runs to align the text on the labels exactly right. This is because most desktop printers are designed to print a certain size of document, typically large pages such as A4.

The variables in the printing process don't usually matter too much: an A4 page may slip a millimetre or so as it goes through the printer without causing problems. That's because exact alignment from one page to the next is rarely required when printing whole A4 pages.

However, when printing labels, small deviations can be disastrous. This is due to the fact that around 20–30 self-adhesive labels are supplied on A4 backing sheets. If there is even a tiny mismatch between the size of each label and the size that your software thinks it is, the error then builds up as successive labels are printed down the page. When this happens, text on the labels towards the bottom of the page might end up overlapping onto the next label, so you'll have to start again.

● Wasting labels

There's also the problem of wastage when you are printing just a couple of labels at a time, in which case you'll be left with a sheet missing the first few labels. The next time you want to print some labels, trying to get your software to ignore these blanks and start on the first label is difficult and time-consuming. You can minimize wastage by turning the page around and starting again, but you'll probably still waste some labels.

Using your regular printer is only feasible if you're doing a long print run of, say, more than 30 labels. If all you want is one label to stick on an envelope, the chances are that all the work involved is just too much hassle and it would be far simpler to handwrite it.

The Matrix II 2003

● The solution

For the home user, the answer is a label printer that can print labels without wastage and frustrating fiddling to get the settings right. These purpose-built machines are small desktop printers that use a continuous roll of labels. They don't print on plain paper and they can't print on A4, so they cannot replace your existing printer. However, they're extremely handy for labels that need to be printed one at a time, such as stickers for envelopes, floppies, files and video tapes, and for printing handy index cards.

Another use for a label printer is to create name badges, particularly for conferences and exhibitions, or just for a party. Label printers at the higher end of the price range can print one label every three seconds, so you needn't worry about waiting for long runs to finish.

One of the other advantages of label printers over ordinary printers is that they use a special thermal printing process. The text is printed by heating the label paper. This means that there is no ink to smudge, should the label get wet. Another bonus is that there's no need for ribbons, inks or toner cartridges. Thermal printing isn't ideal for all printing, but for labels it works well.

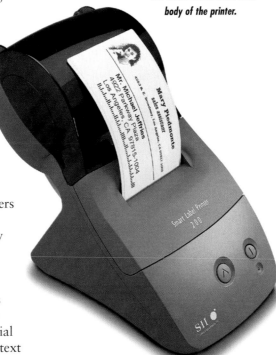

The SLP 200 label printer from Seiko Instruments can print labels up to 54mm wide. Blank labels are stored in the cassette above the main body of the printer.

● Special software

Modern label printers have software that lets you perform a number of special functions. As well as printing whichever typefaces and graphics your software can create, a good label printer will also be able to print barcodes. This is extremely useful if you are running a company that has a barcode-based stock-control system. In addition, you can print the postcode of outgoing letters in barcode form, and this can make a big difference to how fast your mail gets to its destination.

The Seiko range of label printers comes with a contacts program, which allows you to record name and address information from any other piece of software you may have on your computer. You can even print addresses directly from a PalmPilot handheld computer.

Buying a label printer

The most popular type of label printer is made by Seiko (UK tel: 01628 770 988/www.seikosmart.com). There are three SLP (Smart Label Printers) products in the Seiko range. The basic model, the SLP 100 (around £100), is suitable for simple text and graphics, but is fairly slow, taking some eight seconds to print each label. It has a print resolution of 203 dots per inch (dpi), which doesn't match a desktop printer's minimum 300dpi, but is still very respectable. Certainly, this low resolution is adequate for envelopes, floppy disk, video labels and so on.

The next level up is the SLP 200 (approximately £165), which takes around the same time to print labels, and at the same 203dpi resolution. However, its labels are substantially wider than the SLP 100, and thus a better bet for jazzier labels or those with graphics. At the top end is the SLP 240, (around £200), again with the same 203dpi resolution, but which prints labels up to 54mm wide, and at more than twice the speed of the other two models.

Seiko isn't the only company making label printers, but it does seem to be the one most keen on targeting the home computer user and the small/home office market. All three models are network compatible, and so can be shared by a number of users. They also have USB connections, which means you can simply plug them into your computer and get them to work immediately.

If you find it difficult to track down a label printer, your local computer store should be able to help out by ordering one for you.

Three models in the Seiko range of Smart Label Printers are the SLP 100 (left), the SLP 200 (centre) and the SLP 240 (right), which is the top of the SLP range.

Hand-held computers

Once available only to science-fiction characters, the hand-held computer is now a practical reality for anyone who needs to compute on the move. Today's machines pack plenty of computing power into a box that will fit in your pocket.

Hand-held computers add power to your pocket as they not only organize your life, but can also connect you to the Web and allow you to carry huge amounts of information everywhere you go. They've certainly come a long way from their simple name and address – or databank – predecessors, and today's models offer the user real power on the move.

A hand-held computer is ideal for day-to-day use. Wherever you are, you can have instant access to contact details, an electronic notepad, a word processor, a spreadsheet or even games to liven up dull journeys.

● What's inside?

Some hand-held computers have a clamshell design where the protective case opens up to reveal an LCD screen and miniature QWERTY keyboard.

However, if you could look inside at the parts, you'd find some important differences from the computer on your desk. A few parts look the same, and at its heart the hand-held still has a processor and memory, although these use less power than those on a desktop PC to maximize the battery life.

However, there's no hard disk or floppy disk inside a hand-held computer. It relies on its internal memory to store programs and your documents. Some memory – called ROM – is used to store the computer's built-in software permanently. For the data you create, the computer uses RAM. While the hand-held computer is switched off, a tiny amount of back-up battery power is used to store your data.

Of course, the normal computer monitor is replaced with the LCD display in a hand-held version. Although some hand-held computers have small black-and-white screens, larger colour screens are available on an increasing number. Like desktop computers, most hand-held computers can also have hardware plugged into them, perhaps to provide extra memory (see pages 112–115). There's very little space inside, so these add-ons are much smaller. Most hand-helds use PC Cards for add-ons such as modems.

For the ultimate in portable computers, Nokia combines a mobile phone with a modem in its 9210 Communicator.

Keyboards vary considerably from one hand-held computer to another. Not all have keys as large and easy to use as those on the Psion Series 7, shown here.

WHAT IT MEANS

PC CARDS

A PC Card is a plug-in device for portable and hand-held computers. The PC Card is the same size as a credit card, but a lot thicker so it can contain electronic circuits. Some work like miniature hard disks, allowing you to store your documents and new software; others are used for modems.

Different types

The pioneer company in hand-held computing is Psion. From its original 1980s personal organizer, which was styled like a fat calculator, it now offers a powerful blend of hardware, display and built-in software. Its Series 7 and Revo computers come with full software packages, providing word processing and spreadsheets, plus personal organizers and contact books. There are also Web sites from which Psion owners can download lots of additional software.

Windows on the move

Some hand-held computers have a cut-down version of Windows, called Windows for Handheld PC or Pocket PC. These also include built-in versions of Word and Excel in addition to the personal organizer software. Available from Hewlett-Packard, Casio, Toshiba, and other manufacturers, these hand-held computers feature a PC Card slot for adding extra features and a pencil-like pointer to use with the touch screen.

The Nokia Communicator 9210 is a hand-held computer combined with a mobile phone and modem. This means that, in addition to making phone calls, you can send faxes and connect to the Web while on the move (though the high costs of surfing the Internet at mobile phone rates needs to be borne in mind).

The HP Journada is an extremely powerful hand-held computer – shown here in operation in the James Bond film The World is Not Enough.

An increasing number of hand-held computers – such as the Palm series – take a completely different approach. While they offer the usual range of personal organizer software, there's no keyboard at all. You write everything straight on to the screen using the special stylus supplied with the computer.

The systems don't actually recognize handwriting – that would require processing power that hand-held computers just don't have; instead,

Not all hand-held computers use keyboards. With the Palm computer you write directly onto the screen.

you must learn a range of simple symbols in order to input information. In the case of the Palm, for example, the system is called Grafitti.

Living with a hand-held computer

The biggest stumbling block with hand-held computers is the keyboard. It's fine for entering short notes or contact details, but it is very cramped and you would struggle to write long letters. In general, hand-held computers are better thought of as mobile stores of information rather than full-blown computers.

Most hand-helds have two sets of batteries: standard AA-size batteries power the screen and most of the computer's systems and a lithium battery keeps your data safely stored in the computer while the machine is switched off and the main batteries are replaced.

However, for a safer back-up, invest in the necessary cables and software to link your hand-held computer to your desktop PC.

CHECKPOINT ✔

BUYING A HAND-HELD COMPUTER

The most important factor when buying a hand-held computer is to decide what you are going to use it for. This will allow you to quiz your dealer for the answers to the following questions:

☑ **How much memory?**
The ROM and RAM determine how much room there is for the programs and your data – the more the better.

☑ **What software?**
Ask about the built-in software and the range of software that is available on the plug-in cards.

☑ **How much?**
Prices tend to vary a lot, so shop around for the best deal.

☑ **Upgradable?**
Can the computer be upgraded via PC Cards or via software from Web sites?

☑ **PC connectable?**
How does the computer connect to your PC and do you need extra cables for this? For some, the lead is supplied; for others, it can cost an extra £20 or so.

CONNECTING YOUR HAND-HELD COMPUTER TO A DESKTOP PC

Connecting a hand-held computer to your desktop computer is a simple process that can bring many benefits. It takes only a few minutes to link the cable between the two computers and install the special software on your desktop PC.

Once this is done, you can back up any important information stored in your hand-held and transfer files between the two machines. This means that you can write, edit or add to any document on your hand-held computer while on the move and then transfer it to your PC when you get home. If you have Internet access on your desktop computer, you can also use it to find and download new programs – first to your desktop PC and then to your hand-held computer.

Portable add-ons

There are accessories to help you work on the move and make the most of your portable PC. You can print out, fax or email without even plugging into a mains electricity supply.

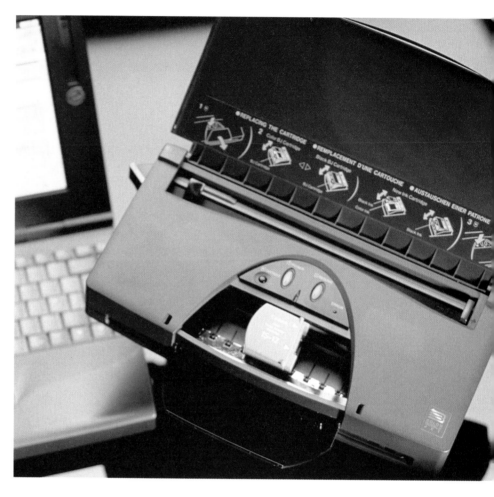

When you're computing on the move, you want to travel as light as possible, but you still need to do most of the things you do at your desktop computer, such as accessing email and printing documents. Fortunately, there's a massive range of peripherals and add-ons for portable PCs – these are designed to help you do all the things you need to while you're away from your desk.

The main reason for buying a notebook or hand-held computer is mobility: you can work in the kitchen at home, take the computer on holiday with you, or work on the train and be able to carry on writing an urgent report in Word or put together a business plan in Excel.

Almost all notebook and hand-held computers can carry out these tasks, but to get the most out of them, you might want to look at add-ons that help to augment the computer's capabilities. Few portable computers come supplied with everything you might need to cover all eventualities while you're out and about, so here is a selection of the most useful.

● The essentials

The most likely things you'll need to do are to print a document and use your email and fax. Many users of portable computers therefore see printers and modems as essential.

While there are many other add-ons you can buy, whether or not you consider them essential will depend almost entirely on the circumstances in which you use your computer. Here we take a look at some of the most popular categories of add-ons for portable computers.

● Keeping in touch

Communications devices – principally modems – are perhaps the most desirable and useful add-ons for owners of older notebook PCs that don't include a built-in modem. The modem lets you send and receive email, faxes and voice messages from a phone point anywhere in the world. Even if your PC has a modem, when you are away from a phone point, you may need a solution that works

with your mobile phone instead of a landline. You have several choices depending on the models of notebook PC and mobile phone you have. Some of the more feature-packed mobile phones have infra-red communication ports. These can communicate directly with the infra-red ports on most notebook PCs.

Using a similar type of signal to that used to adjust your TV by a remote control, these devices set up a connection and transfer data without the need for plugging in any wires. The alternative – the best option if your mobile phone has no infra-red port – is a cable kit; you need to buy one designed specifically to work with your model of mobile phone.

If your portable PC has no modem, it's often worth adding one – even if your mobile phone and notebook can communicate via infra-red. The reason is that landline calls are much cheaper than mobile calls, and the modem will quickly pay for itself. For business users, a network adaptor allows the computer to connect to an office network.

What you don't want for your portable computer, of course, is a modem the size of the one you are quite happy to have on your desktop because it might well be almost as bulky as the portable computer itself. Fortunately, the large-scale adoption in recent years of the PCMCIA standard for credit card-sized devices, now more widely known as PC Cards, means that portable users are spoilt for choice when it comes to small, lightweight modems and communications peripherals.

With the BJC-85 printer from Canon you can travel anywhere and always have the ability to print high-quality documents, even in colour. Don't forget to take a supply of paper with you, though!

DIFFERENT PC CARD TYPES

There are three kinds of PC Cards: Type I, Type II and Type III. All have the same rectangular dimensions of 8.5cm by 5.5cm, but the thicknesses differ: 3.3mm for Type I, 5.5mm for Type II and 10.5mm for Type III.

The thicker PC Cards accommodate bigger components, including miniature hard disks. Portable computers usually have two PC Card slots into which these devices slide. Once they are fitted, and any special software is installed, the cards work in exactly the same way as any other internal component of the computer.

Most portable computers offer the user a choice of one Type III slot, or two Type II slots (Type I is rarely seen nowadays). A Type III slot will accept a Type II card, but not vice versa. Most current PC Card modems and related devices are Type II.

Nearly all the major modem suppliers, such as 3Com and Intel's Xircom, offer PC Card modems. Prices are generally around the £50 mark for a 56Kbps PCMCIA modem card.

● Advanced communications

For some of the more sophisticated communications features, such as an office network adaptor and/or an adaptor for your mobile phone, you'll pay rather more. For example, anything between £100 and £200 is not unusual, depending on the number of features involved. Note that to use a portable computer with a standard mobile phone, you'll also need a special connector cable that is often specific to a particular model of phone. Check the phone's manual for details.

One point to bear in mind if you're planning to travel abroad with a portable and modem is that phone sockets vary from country to country. Few things are more frustrating than finding that you cannot plug your

Hand-held add-ons

Just as there are many add-ons that make life easier with a notebook PC, so there are similar add-ons that add extra features to many hand-held computers. These tend to be even smaller and more ingenious. For example, with Palm computers you input data by moving the stylus on the touch-sensitive screen – a good idea but potentially frustrating for entering large amounts of text. By adding a portable keyboard, however, you can type text in instead. Remarkably the keyboard folds up into a pocket-sized package.

Other useful hand-held accessories include extra styli – typically a few pounds each – and connectivity kits for Internet access. Space is at such a premium in hand-held computers that the PC Card slot that is a must-have for notebook PCs, is too big. Instead hand-helds usually come with a smaller slot that takes accessories which provide many of the same features in a smaller package.

Bluetooth devices are available which use radio technology to enable wireless communication, thereby allowing hand-held computer to 'talk' to your printer or desktop PC without any wires at all.

modem into a waiting socket. However, you can easily get round this problem by taking a modem travel kit with you, which will allow you to plug into phone systems worldwide. Such kits cost around £50–£60.

● Printers
The paperless office remains only a dream and is likely to do so for the foreseeable future. Someone, somewhere is always going to expect a hard copy of a document or a paper fax rather than an email. Therefore if you're out and about with your laptop, you might well be able to do any printing you need from offices or homes you visit. However, if you know that you'll regularly need to print documents, you should consider buying yourself a portable printer.

These are surprisingly compact and lightweight, and typically use inkjet printing technology. As a result, you can print in black and white or colour. They also give you the option of using special battery packs, so you are not reliant on having power sockets nearby.

● Portability
The main attraction of these portable printers remains their small size. Canon's BJC-85, for example, weighs in at a mere 1.4kg (around 3.25lb) and is only 30cm wide by 16cm deep by 6cm high. With these dimensions it doesn't really add too much bulk to what you have to carry around with you. Portable printers are available at

a moderate price; for around £160–£200 you can purchase such popular models as the Canon BJC-85 or the HP DeskJet 350.

Some printers have the same type of infra-red communications ports as those mentioned on the previous page. An infra-red port on a notebook computer can transmit the image of the page to the infra-red port on the printer, doing away with the need for a cable.

● Power options
Power is always at a premium with a portable computer, no matter how good your batteries. Whenever possible, you should use an external power supply and conserve precious battery power for when it is really needed. Most portables are supplied with an AC/DC adaptor as standard but, as with modems, if you are travelling abroad you should invest in an international socket adaptor to make sure your power supply is compatible. Many notebook PC users invest in an extra battery so that they can work for longer periods away from the mains supply. You'll get the best price if you buy one with your notebook, but you can also buy extra batteries from around £60.

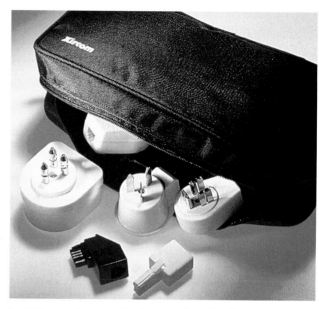

Intel's Xircom produces convenient international travel kits for your modem-equipped portable PC. These kits allow you to connect to electrical sockets and phone systems wherever you are in the world.

● Storage
Hard disk drives, CD-ROM drives and floppy drives are all heavy components that take up a relatively large amount of space, so notebook computers rarely have all the storage options of desktop machines, or the large hard disk capacities. Storage space is therefore always an issue for users of portable computers.

With smaller portable PCs – sometimes called 'sub-notebooks' – you might have only a hard disk built into the case. On larger portables, you will find a CD-ROM drive or a floppy disk drive as standard, in addition to the hard drive. On some models the CD-ROM drive is interchangeable with a floppy disk drive: you simply swap the units around, depending on which one you need to use.

Whatever configuration you have, you will probably want to have some

ADDING A KEYBOARD AND MOUSE

One of the compromises you must make when you buy a notebook computer is the size of the keyboard – a notebook computer usually manages with around 80–90 keys instead of the full desktop complement of 102 keys.

The keys are also slightly smaller and don't travel quite as far when you press them. If you miss the typing action or the numeric keypad of a full-size computer keyboard, add one using the keyboard socket or a USB port. Just plug a keyboard into the socket located at the rear of the notebook – no extra software is needed.

If you use your notebook mainly at home and very rarely on the move, the £10–£20 invested in a desktop keyboard could certainly be worthwhile.

You can also add a conventional mouse to your notebook computer to replace the trackball or finger pad. Adding it is as easy as plugging a mouse into a desktop computer and, at around £15, it's another low-cost and effective add-on. Your notebook computer's manual will give you guidance on the presence of external keyboard, mouse and USB sockets as well as any special fitting instructions.

If your notebook PC doesn't have a CD drive, an external CD-RW drive that connects via USB is a powerful and cost-effective addition.

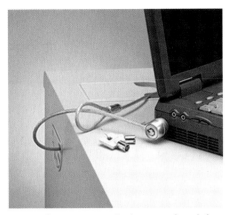

Secure and protect your notebook computer from theft with a portable security kit. Insert the lock in the security slot in your portable computer and wrap the steel cable to any immovable object.

means of transferring files, other than by email. Perhaps the best option is an external Zip drive (see Stage 3, pages 98–99). Zip drives are quite small and light, while the disks have a capacity of up to 250MB – the equivalent of more than 175 standard floppy disks.

Zip drives are increasingly common in homes and offices and are fitted as standard on some desktop computers, so there is a very good chance that you will be able to swap data with most users.

External Zip drives cost around £100, while the disks are around £10 each. If you don't have a CD-ROM drive built into your notebook and find that you need one, you can get an external lightweight CD-ROM or CD-RW drive, specifically designed for use with portables, for around £100–£150. These drives are slimline, weigh around 0.5kg (1lb) and connect to your computer via the PC Card slot (or via the USB port).

This motion-detecting alarm detects movements and goes off at a volume of about 100db.

Those who are serious computer users and need massive extra storage options, should consider an external hard drive. Rather than using a conventional hard disk, look for PC card disks when travelling. A 5GB PC card hard disk costs around £250, but cheaper, smaller capacity cards can be found.

● Security
Computer theft is on the increase and portables are a prime target. Vigilance is the best safeguard against theft so, if possible, never let your portable out of your sight. Clearly, though, there will be occasions when this is not possible. Most portable computers have a built-in security retention slot which allows you to attach one end of a lockable steel cable to the computer and the other to an immovable object, such as a heavy table or filing cabinet. These devices are simple and relatively cheap at around £40.

There are also plenty of alternative systems available, for example, the Kensington SonicLock motion-detecting alarm, which costs about £25. You attach it to a carrying case, or use the notebook adapter to connect it to your laptop, and then alarm it using the three-digit key pad; the alarm will activate at the slightest bump or jiggle.

● Portable comfort
When you're actually on the move, you'll want something that provides

An inexpensive, soft-sided case (below) might be fine, but it won't offer much protection or extra storage space.

comfort for you and protection for the computer. There is a vast range of portable carrying cases available. Prices start at around £20–£30.

At the bottom end of the price range there are some perfectly acceptable padded cases. However, you can purchase something a little more spacious, possibly with a rigid shell, for around £60–£70. An alternative to this, and at a similar price, is a case that offers extra protection in the form of a pressurized air bag which surrounds the computer. The engineering used to create the case is based on the way a racing car chassis absorbs energy to protect the driver in a crash. As you'll come to depend on your portable it makes sense to give it as much protection as possible.

If your portable computer is in a case surrounded by pressurized air, it is theoretically protected in drops of up to 2 metres.

Upgrading your speakers

Improving your speakers is an easy, five-minute job, with the reward of deeper sound for your music CDs and your games' soundtracks. If you're serious about Multimedia, here's how to get more bass.

Although your PC probably came with a pair of speakers, it's unlikely they are particularly powerful or of a high quality. They were, after all, bundled with the PC, and manufacturers give greater consideration to the small amount of desktop space they take up rather than their sound quality.

Standard PC speakers tend to be relatively quiet, tinny and have a poor frequency range. In particular, their small size limits the diameter of the speakers inside: the smaller the size, the poorer the bass response. Consequently, Multimedia programs – and particularly games – can sound rather harsh and lifeless.

● Pump up the bass

One solution is to buy a better pair of speakers, but although this will certainly help, the central problem remains: speakers with a really good bass output are too big to sit on your desktop. The best solution is to upgrade to a speaker set-up that includes a sub-woofer. This is a specially designed amplifier and speaker. Sub-woofers can take up a lot of space, but they can usually be placed beneath the desk while the smaller desktop speakers remain next to your PC (see PC Tips, opposite).

If all you want is better quality for playing music CDs and MP3s on your PC, you can opt for a low-cost package of a pair of speakers with a sub-woofer. You need spend no more than £40 or so. However, if you are

likely to be playing a lot of games on your PC, it may be worth upgrading to a surround-sound set-up.

● Behind you!

The most successful games are those that combine good gameplay with a compelling atmosphere. In the same way that a surround-sound TV helps to immerse you in a movie, extra sound channels on your PC help to put you right into the centre of the game's scenario. Being able to hear your opponents coming up behind you is really helpful, whether you're racing Formula 1 cars or trying to avoid flesh-eating zombies.

Before choosing which speaker upgrade route to take, you also need

to consider your PC's sound card. Surround sound requires a surround-sound capable sound card (see Sound cards box, below).

SOUND CARDS

You can upgrade any PC with a sound card to a sub-woofer system. It uses the same socket that your current desktop speakers use (shown opposite). However, if you want to upgrade to a full surround-sound system, you must also have a sound card that can decode the surround sound data and send the appropriate signals to each speaker. Examples include the SoundBlaster Audigy cards. Check your PC's documentation if you're not sure if your sound card can play surround sound.

Adding a sub-woofer and speaker set-up

If you find the sound quality from your PC speakers is tinny or harsh, get closer to hi-fi sound quality by upgrading to a speaker set-up that includes a sub-woofer.

1 Before you install any new hardware you should make sure your computer is turned off and the power plug taken out at the wall. Remember: your speakers probably have their own power supply to turn off and unplug at the mains point.

2 At the rear of your computer, locate the lead that links your sound card to your speakers. Remove this and your speakers.

3 Follow the connection instructions supplied with your new speakers. In this example, the cable from the PC sound card connects directly to the socket on the back of the sub-woofers which makes the installation a very straightforward process.

4 Now make the other speaker signal connections. Typically you must first connect a lead from the sub-woofer to one of the desktop speakers and connect another cable between both of the two speakers. These plugs are often colour-coded to make things easy.

5 You can position the sub-woofer almost anywhere. On our model, there are controls on the sub-woofer, so it makes sense to keep it close to hand. Finally, connect up the speakers' power supply and switch everything on. Play a music CD and adjust the speaker controls to get a good balance between the sub-woofer and desktop speakers.

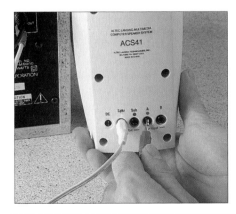

PC TIPS

The sub-woofer is fairly large, so you may not want to put it on your desktop. Most people usually put it under the desk. The problem with this is that the sub-woofer can make an awful lot of noise and vibration, so be aware of this if there are people on the floor below who could be disturbed.

When deciding where to place the sub-woofer, also bear in mind where the volume controls are located. If they are on the sub-woofer, rather than the desktop speakers, you may need to keep it close by.

Home Learning & Leisure

Biology revision aids

The onset of exams is always a stressful time, but with Multimedia revision aids the student can relax more and practise in a familiar environment at his or her own pace.

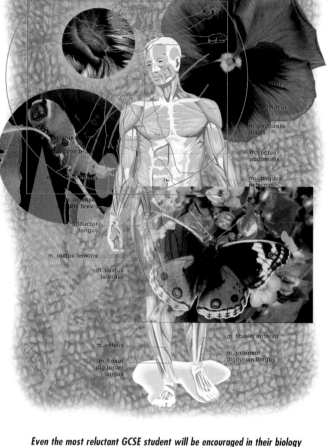

Even the most reluctant GCSE student will be encouraged in their biology studies if they use a Multimedia CD-ROM.

There are some excellent Multimedia revision aids available and GCSE biology is no exception. We've looked at other revision aid titles in *PCs made easy* (see Stage 1, pages 118-119), so you won't be surprised to learn that there's a wide choice of products available.

What's slightly different with biology though is that, as a science, it can be approached on its own or together with chemistry and physics. This is reflected in the products we look at here: one is a single-topic CD, while the other is part of a set. Obviously, your choice will depend on which subjects you're studying.

GCSE Biology, from Dorling Kindersley, is everything you would expect from this publisher. It's solidly thought out, easy to follow and well presented. In common with other titles in the Dorling Kindersley Multimedia range (now published by GSP), *GCSE Biology* is test-based, offering more than 1,000 questions, all of which are written by practising teachers.

The program can be customized to the student's particular exam board and it spans the entire biology syllabus at GCSE Key Stage 4 (14–16 year olds). The program is broken down into modules under the four main headings: Processes of Life, Reproduction and Inheritance, Ecology, and Diet and Digestion.

● A question of choice

There's a clever slider bar at each level so that you can specify how many questions you want to answer on any given subject, up to the given total. This provides you with complete control over the tests, allowing you to concentrate on any chosen area.

It's probably wise to leave a few questions unanswered in any category, so that you can give yourself a complete, all-round test at the end of your revision. You can easily keep track of what you've done via the Progress section of the Main menu, which also allows you to complete any unfinished tests.

The questions themselves are set in a multiple choice format and once you have given the correct answer, the program offers a clear and comprehensive explanation of it. So, even if you picked the correct answer by guessing, you will learn to answer the question correctly next time.

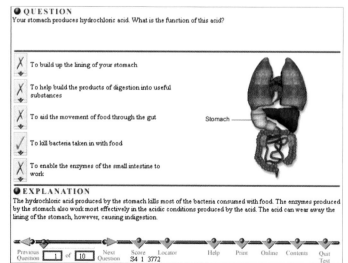

The multiple choice interface in Dorling Kindersley's GCSE Biology is clear and colourful. Once you have answered a question correctly, it gives you more detailed information about it.

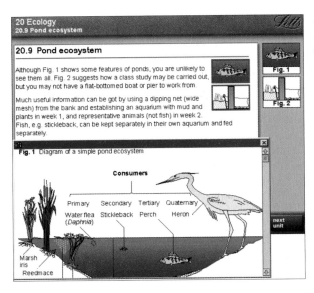

20 Ecology
20.9 Pond ecosystem

20.9 Pond ecosystem

Although Fig. 1 shows some features of ponds, you are unlikely to see them all. Fig. 2 suggests how a class study may be carried out, but you may not have a flat-bottomed boat or pier to work from.

Much useful information can be got by using a dipping net (wide mesh) from the bank and establishing an aquarium with mud and plants in week 1, and representative animals (not fish) in week 2. Fish, e.g. stickleback, can be kept separately in their own aquarium and fed separately.

Fig. 1 Diagram of a simple pond ecosystem

Consumers

Primary, Secondary, Tertiary, Quaternary
Water flea (*Daphnia*), Stickleback, Perch, Heron

Marsh iris
Reedmace

Fig. 1
Fig. 2
next unit

Here's a representative revision course screen from Letts Revise for GCSE Biology *(left). Detailed explanations for each topic are accompanied by small graphics. Click on the graphics to see a more detailed labelled diagram.*

Test yourself in The Times Education GCSE Biology *(below) by dragging your answers to the correct annotation boxes. Then check if you got it right by clicking on the Check answer button at the bottom.*

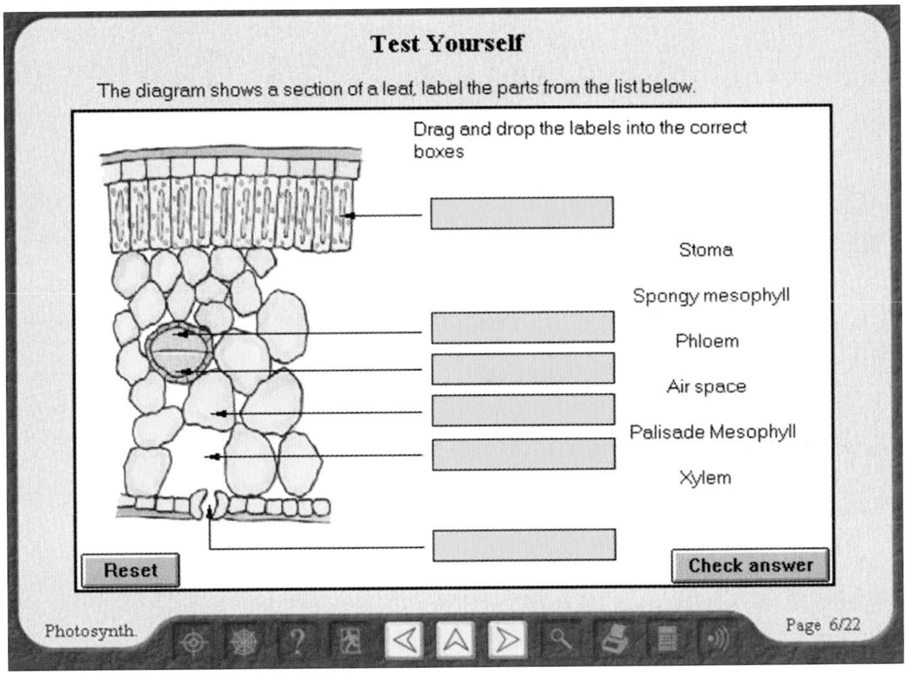

Test Yourself

The diagram shows a section of a leaf, label the parts from the list below.

Drag and drop the labels into the correct boxes

Stoma
Spongy mesophyll
Phloem
Air space
Palisade Mesophyll
Xylem

Reset   Check answer

Photosynth.   Page 6/22

There are more than 800 attractive graphics, enlivened by the occasional 3D animation. A running score is kept throughout, which also provides handy analysis of your strengths and weaknesses. The program has a useful logging-on procedure, whereby you have to identify yourself and give a password, allowing more than one person to use the software to revise for the same exam. Crucially, this ensures that one student's progress isn't confused with another's.

● **Exam success**
Letts Revise for GCSE Biology, like the Dorling Kindersley program, is aimed at Key Stage 4 students and it, too, is customizable, depending on which GCSE syllabus you are taking.

The program is relentlessly goal-driven – the goal, of course, is to pass the GCSE exam with a good grade.

When you log in for the first time you have to give the current date and the date of your first exam, the number of subjects you are taking and the total amount of time per week you are intending to devote to revision. It is, of course, best to be honest with yourself here and not exaggerate your good intentions.

If you don't know how to go about revising then this program will supply a wealth of practical and valuable tips. You'll find out, for example, what the optimum amount of revision in any given session should be, and how often you need to test yourself as the exams draw nearer.

The core of the software, however, is made up of the revision course and the progress tests. Based on the syllabus you selected when logging in, the software gives a thorough and well-illustrated presentation of all the information you need to pass your Biology GCSE. Topics are presented with a text explanation in the main window and one or two diagrams to the right; you should click on these to view more detailed information. The text explanations are clear and easy-to-follow, and there are also some animations to liven up your study.

When you've completed your revision, you can proceed to the Test Your Progress section. If you haven't mastered a topic this will soon become evident – and you'll be given a chance to repeat the revision modules again.

● **Read up on it**
The Times Education GCSE Biology is not quite so relentless in its approach, offering a more patient delivery as the student gains exam confidence. It covers all of the key curriculum topics including life processes and green plants, humans as organisms, and variation, inheritance and evolution. This is backed up with self-testing routines and solid revision techniques.

All of these packages are frequently updated to take account of the fact that syllabuses change regularly, so if you use them properly you should have no excuse for not passing your exams.

CONTACT POINTS

Dorling Kindersley GCSE Biology
Price: £19.99*
Letts Revise for GCSE Biology
Price: £19.99*
GSP
Tel: 01480 496666
www.gsp.cc

The Times Education GCSE Biology
Price: £14.99*
Idigicon
Tel: 01302 314000
www.idigicon.com

*UK prices

Ancient civilizations

With a host of excellent Multimedia titles, your computer can help to bring history to life and give you a deeper understanding of the development of civilization – from Ancient Egypt to the Roman Empire.

History's Great Civilisations *from GSP begins in this den of archeological finds, with a voiceover leading you into each of the topic areas for further exploration.*

One great advantage of Multimedia as a learning aid is its potential to bring its subject to life. Ancient history is a good example, as shown on a number of CD-ROMs through their use of interactive maps, time lines and animated reconstructions.

Nowadays, early history is an important subject area in schools, especially at primary level, but it holds a fascination for all ages.

● Voyage to the past

History's Great Civilisations packs four popular areas of study into one. Starting from an archeologist's den, animations and an explanatory voice-over introduce you to the ancient worlds of Troy, Pompeii, Persepolis and Tutankhamen's Egypt.

From here, you will be taken on a fascinating journey around the cities and culture of each of these ancient civilizations. Each site is presented as a 3D reconstruction for you to explore, along with detailed maps and chronological tables. Particularly enthralling, for example, is the tour

around Tutankhamen's tomb, where you will learn all about the various treasures found there.

If you prefer, you can delve into the CD-ROM's background information database to locate the topics you are most interested in. In the database are more than 100 pages of text and a vast repository of photos that detail the events, origins, art and locations of the civilisations covered. This material can be copied and pasted into student projects or printed out.

The comprehensive coverage of this title, packing four topics into one product, makes it great value for money but for more detailed information on individual civilizations, you might prefer to try one of the single-topic titles.

● Learning through games

A single-topic approach is demonstrated in *Ancient Egyptians* and *Ancient Greeks* from Granada Learning – two educational games created for the National Curriculum.

Ancient Egyptians takes a whistle-stop tour through Egyptian history and is based around an interface showing hieroglyphic symbols on two walls. Those on the left represent periods of history. Clicking on these symbols calls up a commentary, with the main points bulleted like revision notes.

The other symbols represent the cast of characters which includes a priest, a farmer, a noble lady and a pharaoh. Clicking on these is much more fun because the symbols transform into video animations, which tell you about day-to-day life in ancient Egypt. The subjects covered range from mummies to farming and are presented in the same easy-to-follow bullet points. The heart of the game is

This is the temple of Zeus, and it is here that we came to worship our gods, but chiefly Zeus, king of the gods...   More...

Granada Learning's Ancient Greeks *involves you in the rebuilding of a ruined city, after which you can explore the houses, temples and many other buildings.*

In Ancient Egyptians, from Granada Learning, a video pharaoh introduces a variety of topics, which are then broken down into simple, memorable explanations.

a treasure hunt in which you try to free the soul of the dead pharaoh. You have to interact with the cast to find missing items, completing puzzles as you go. The game ends as the pharaoh becomes one with the gods. It's an interesting, well-presented CD-ROM with an absorbing and different approach to this subject.

● Greeks and Romans

Ancient Greeks recreates everyday life in a typical city of the era, again with a video guide character who explains what you need to do and relates what it was like to live in those days. She even tests you on your knowledge with a number of fun quizzes. Once you have rebuilt the ancient ruins of the city, they can be explored. Alternatively, you can skip straight to other topics such as myths and legends, sports and theatre.

As well as the CD-ROMs themselves, Granada Learning can provide school teachers' editions of *Ancient Egyptians* and *Ancient*

Greeks, complete with printed notes and printable worksheets to enhance the lessons for the students.

Jumping in time and space to the ancient Roman Empire, *Pompeii Interactive* from Canis Education is a very different type of CD-ROM. Rather than trying to reconstruct the doomed city as it looked before Vesuvius erupted, this title is a tour of the city ruins as they appear today.

Alongside the comprehensive range of photographic records is an explanation of every building and locality in ancient Pompeii, how they were used or occupied, and an introduction to key events and contemporary culture.

Unlike the other CD-ROMs featured here, *Pompeii Interactive* is designed to run in any Web browser. You can even preview the title online before buying (see Contact Points).

The Ancient World Web (above) has over 1,200 sites listed by category.

Pompeii Interactive (right) takes you on a tour of the famous ancient ruined city as it looks today, with every area photographed from multiple aspects.

CONTACT POINTS

History's Great Civilisations
Price: £9.99*
GSP
Tel: 01480 496666
www.gsp.cc

Ancient Egyptians
Price: £20 (£49 with teachers' notes)*
Ancient Greeks
Price: £20 (£49 with teachers' notes)*
Granada Learning
Tel: 0161 827 2927
www.granada-learning.com

Pompeii Interactive
Price: £45*
Canis Education
www.pompeii.co.uk

*UK prices

SITES TO @ VISIT

There is a wealth of information available on the Internet, and the sheer variety and detail can be impressive. Here's one excellent link to many sites:

Ancient World Web (AWW)
This is maintained by one person for no commercial gain. Created and managed by Julia Hayden, it lists hundreds of sites by region and by subject. Most impressively, it gives a précis and critical appreciation of what each one has to offer:
www.julen.net/ancient/

Manage your money

If your accounts are in a mess and you've lost track of what you've been spending, you may need the help of money management software to solve your financial problems.

Managing personal and household finances is a task we all have to do, but very few people enjoy it. Many of us are inefficient when it comes to organising our finances, keeping important paperwork in all sorts of different places, not examining the state of our savings and investments, and forgetting to pay bills. Financial management is important and becomes even more so if you're running a small business.

● **Financial management software**
However, help is at hand in the shape of financial management software. Such software has been around since the dawn of computers and has been widely used in business for many years. Large companies need to know how much cash they have, who is late paying their bills and how much VAT or tax is due in any given period. Managers need up-to-date reports on all aspects of the company finances so that they can make plans for the future. Until the 1980s, software that could do all this ran on large

computers only, which were regularly maintained and updated by technical and financial experts.

With the arrival of affordable and powerful PCs, however, the kind of power that was once the privilege of big business is now available at home. Programs such as Quicken and Microsoft Money can really put you in control of your outgoings, income and savings.

These programs can give you instant reports on the state of your overall finances or on any given aspect, such as your mortgage, savings or investments. With the increasing use of the Internet as a business tool, some types of financial management software will even let

Take most of the paper out of your paperwork – prepare your accounts by using a financial management program.

you connect via the Web to your bank, download your statement and then use it in the software.

Most personal finance programs are updated each year to reflect changes in taxation and other fast-developing areas, such as online banking. However, the basic approach of the programs remains the same. The Microsoft Money series offers very similar functions to Intuit's Quicken range. At the core of the programs are very powerful accounting abilities.

● **A good account of yourself**
When you start using a financial management program you must enter all the financial details relating

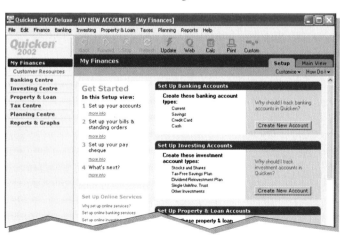

Intuit Quicken's setup page provides lots of helpful advice on getting started and lets you gradually build your accounts information at your own pace.

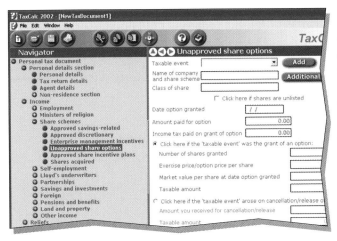

TaxCalc (created by Which Software and sold by Intuit) makes filling in your tax return a much easier process, using a Windows Explorer-style navigation system to travel between different forms.

to the different categories of your expenditure and income. The more information you provide, the better.

If you are using Microsoft Money, a powerful Wizard will help you to set up various accounts, as needed. The type of account can be selected from a list covering pretty much everything you might need, including investments, house, loan, and so forth. Setting up your account is an easy process, although be aware that you must gather all the relevant documents, such as mortgage details and bank statements, so that you have the information to hand.

If you enter information about a recurring transaction – a monthly loan repayment, for example – Money automatically detects it as such, allowing you to enter it into the Bill Calendar, which will pop up with a reminder when payments fall due. You can also handle savings and investments just as easily as outgoings, setting up an account for different stock portfolios, for example. Money can even update your investment portfolios via its Internet connection. Another function most people will find useful is the lifetime planning. Tell Money what your target is and it will produce a plan based on the data you have entered.

● Chart your finances
Finally, Money has powerful reporting and charting facilities, which can help to give you a clear picture of where any given part, or all, of your finances stand. You can create regular monthly reports showing where the money comes from and where it goes, or you can produce specific reports and charts on, say, the performance of your investments and savings. It's this ability to produce a clear financial picture at the click of a button that really makes financial software worth the effort for the home user.

● Taxing times
One piece of financial management that comes round without fail every year is your annual tax return. With the introduction of Self Assessment, filling in your form correctly and sending it in on time are more important than ever.

To many people this is an extremely daunting task, but this is where you need tax calculation software, such as TaxCalc from Which Software. This program takes you through the entire process, starting with an 'interview' in which you enter all the relevant details into the boxes. The software then works out your tax liability for you. It also provides tips on how you can legitimately minimize liabilities.

The Inland Revenue accepts a print-out from TaxCalc as a valid document, thus saving you the task of filling in forms by hand, and making it much easier to complete on time.

At work
Financial management software can help take the strain out of running a business.

It's absolutely crucial to know where you stand with your finances if you are running a small business. This is because there are legal obligations to pay tax, National Insurance and VAT. Even the smallest business needs accurate, detailed financial data to plan for the future. No wonder that the birth of the computer was accompanied by the introduction of accounting software. The popular Instant Accounts software from Sage reproduces the traditional book-keeping structure of sales, purchase and nominal ledgers but gives you a lot more besides. On the basis of information entered on sales and purchases, the software will calculate VAT and generate invoices and reports. Instant Accounts is suitable for small businesses of up to about 10 employees.

Instant Accounts requires little knowledge of accounting. Pop-up windows are easy to work with and there's a plethora of Wizards to help you set up accounts.

Formula 1 racing

Lightning-fast computers are used to monitor and enhance the speed and performance of racing cars, helping them to become quicker than ever before.

The cars used in Formula 1 racing exhibit all the characteristics of modern high-technology: incredible speed, an inspired mix of analogue and digital systems and that hyper-streamlined shape. Each of these attributes is largely due to the modern Formula 1 car being designed, created – and even partly driven – by computer technology.

The computer's involvement in Formula 1 starts at the very beginning, when the design of the car is conceived. Because computers are now so powerful, and computer-aided design (CAD) is widely used in the industry, it is actually quite some time before a new car design is moved from the virtual drawing-board to the engineering shop.

● Co-ordinated by computer

A wide range of companies is responsible for creating components on a car, most notably the engine, suspension, brakes and tyres. The computer is particularly useful in co-ordinating this work, as high-speed data links and videoconferencing facilities enable companies to interact quickly and efficiently. This way, the

Behind the scenes during a race, a team of technicians watch screens that show all the readings from the racing car's telemetry.

the latest versions of each component are instantly available to the team. Perhaps the most important design work undertaken by the racing team is in the chassis and outer body shell. The design and testing are done on the computer, until the final design has been all but approved, and the model is then tested in a wind tunnel.

The CAD work begins with the car's chassis. While all Formula 1 cars might look pretty much the same to

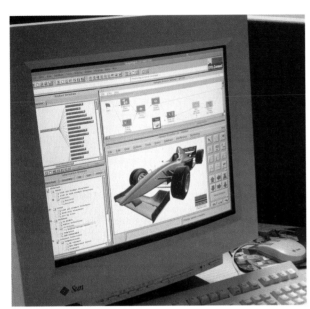

Modern racing cars are among the highest of high-tech products and need sophisticated CAD systems to design each of their numerous components.

The actual types of computer used in Formula 1 vary according to the job in hand. PCs are widely employed during the design process but UNIX-based workstations are often preferred because of the huge amounts of data involved. This is most obvious at the McLaren team, which is sponsored by Sun, a maker of such computers. These computers monitor the timing of cars and races, while others retrieve and correlate telemetry data. McLaren even uses programs written in Sun's Java language to translate data transmitted during the race.

untutored eyes, even the tiniest detail can make a huge difference to a car's performance. For example, in 1998 the FIA (the body controlling motor racing) ordered that all Formula 1 cars should have a 10 per cent reduction in their width. In 2002, the concept of weight handicaps was first raised. These issues have a massive effect on the aerodynamics and material build of a car, and thus its speed.

● Aerodynamics

While building a chassis is a relatively simple task, due to the restrictions enforced by the FIA, the real skill comes in creating the body shell. Not only does it have to be as aerodynamic as possible, it also has to be the optimum shape for fast braking and helping with downforce and grip. The design of the body shell has to take these factors into account – and the best way to see the effect of these design changes is by simulating them on the computer, which speeds up the design process and keeps down costs.

All these different areas of design work take place concurrently, making the computer a necessity for organizing and centralizing the data. Nearly all the car's mechanical components are controlled by computer, enabling the pit crew to monitor the condition of the car by radio signal (known as telemetry), and to respond to any damage or breakdown by preparing replacements in the pits and devising a new race

strategy. Displays in the cockpit also inform the driver of any problems, so that appropriate action can be taken. The responsiveness of the car is helped by the use of computers, with little of the actual cockpit interface controlled by cables or wires. This allows for quicker control of the mechanics. In addition, the gears, brakes, and steering wheel are all controlled by electronics, allowing for relatively minuscule amendments which can result in a significant improvement.

● On track

Once the car gets out onto the race track, the computer's job is far from finished. To fine-tune the various systems, the car is raced on a test circuit to monitor its performance in various conditions. Telemetry data is then recorded from each of the computerized systems. The team can examine the performance of each component, from brakes to gears and optimize them for the coming race.

Just as supercomputing has led to many improvements in desktop computer technology, the technology used in Formula 1 racing will eventually bring about advances in safety, control and diagnostics for the everyday driver as the findings are adopted by standard car manufacturers.

Computer manufacturers sponsor Formula 1 teams because the images of speed, precision and reliability support their marketing messages.

There is one other important way in which computers – and personal computers in particular – are used in Formula 1 racing. Many of the top drivers, including David Coulthard and former Grand Prix champion Jacques Villeneuve, have admitted to using computer games to practise and hone their racing skills. The simulation of choice is the Geoff Crammond's Grand Prix series from Infogrames, now on version 4. Over the years this has remained the top PC simulation, far ahead of its rivals in terms of accuracy and control. Jacques Villeneuve, in particular, found the game very useful, as he was able to use it during his first season to 'practise' on upcoming tracks that he had never raced on before.

You can find out more about the game – and how it is constantly updated to give new features mirroring the real world – at the official www.grandprixgames.com site, or at www.grandprix4.com, a very good unofficial site.

Birds of Europe

If you want to identify a particular species of bird, the most obvious way to do so is to observe the animal's plumage and colouring, and then to look it up in a reference book. However, as any 'twitcher' (birdwatcher) will tell you, distinctive flight patterns and inherent calls are equally important means of identification. This is where the birdwatcher's CD-ROM beats a guidebook hands down.

By adding movement, sound and informative voice-overs to the standard fare of photographs, maps and illustrations, the Multimedia package can do all that a book can do – and much, much more. So, not surprisingly, there are several excellent and creatively produced ornithology CDs available, catering for every level of interest and age group.

● Virtual ornithology

The AA Interactive Encyclopedia of British & European Birds is a concise and affordable beginner's guide to birdwatching. Instead of presenting the information in a conventional, but dull, database or book format, the CD-ROM takes the form of a 3D bird sanctuary. A conservatory houses an Ecology Room, an Avarium, an Information Room and a Games Room, while outside there is a virtual Hide. You are free to wander around these areas, clicking on anything that takes your fancy.

If, however, you prefer a more structured approach, or if you find the interface a little confusing, you can select a list of topics and simply click on them to access the information you would like to see.

The core of the CD-ROM is the bird guide, which presents the 427 species of bird that breed in, or regularly inhabit, Britain and the rest of Europe. However, the complete package will also help you to learn about bird conservation and habitats, the distribution of species throughout

Multimedia products can put some added fun into just about any subject, but you might be surprised to learn that one of the topics to which it is best suited is birdwatching.

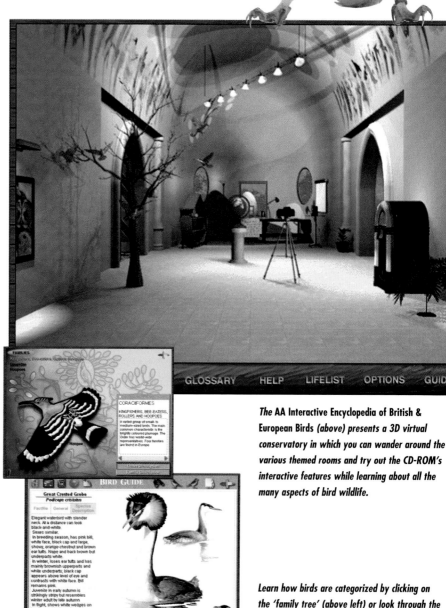

The AA Interactive Encyclopedia of British & European Birds (above) presents a 3D virtual conservatory in which you can wander around the various themed rooms and try out the CD-ROM's interactive features while learning about all the many aspects of bird wildlife.

Learn how birds are categorized by clicking on the 'family tree' (above left) or look through the comprehensive information about specific species in the Bird Guide (left).

Europe (illustrated by attractive maps), the evolution and survival of birds, and a host of other topics.

The information is presented in some depth, accompanied by excellent illustrations. There are 90 video clips on the CD and recordings of more than 500 bird songs. Combine these with the illustrations and the fact file and you have a very good chance of identifying any birds you see when you are out and about with your binoculars in Britain and many other European countries.

● Authoritative information

The dedicated birdwatcher looking for even meatier information should consider the range of titles from BirdGuides. The *CD-ROM Concise Guide to British Birds* is a good introduction to the series, covering common birds of gardens, farmland, wetlands and coasts.

You can expand your knowledge further with a companion title, the *CD-ROM Guide to Rarer British Birds*. Here you can trawl detailed information on 240 rare species, complete with more than 330 video clips. Presented in a simple format running in your Web browser, this title is aimed at the serious amateur, rather than the entertainment seeker.

● Britain and Europe

For the ultimate in PC-based British ornithology though, BirdGuides publishes a set of flagship products for the expert and serious birdwatcher. The *CD-ROM Guide to British Birds* is a two-disc mine of information, but still every bit a Multimedia title in its own right. In a multi-paned window, you can access photographs, detailed

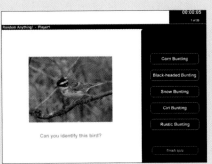

The Guide to British Birds and the Guide to All the Birds of Europe both employ a split-screen presentation in which you can call up detailed drawings, videos and distribution maps.

Test yourself against the clock with a series of timed quizzes (below). Choose one of the topic-specific games or try out the quiz.

drawings, geographical distribution maps, birdsong recordings and over 330 species captured in good quality video footage. One of the especially interesting features is the ability to compare two species side-by-side using the multi-paned layout.

The title is not an introduction to birdwatching, but a working tool for the practising ornithologist. The package includes a Bird Log for keeping track of your own regular sightings, and a handy 'What bird was that?' wizard to help you identify birds you may not have seen before.

An expanded edition is also available: the *CD-ROM Guide to All the Birds of Europe*. This is a six-disc set in the same style as the *British Birds* title but covering more than 600 species in text, image and video. For your convenience, both

guides are sold in an alternative DVD-ROM format, where everything fits on to just one disc. Additionally, you can ensure you always have the latest information by downloading the free updates available on the BirdGuides Web site at www.birdguides.com.

The Lists From Maps feature (below) finds bird species according to the areas you indicate on a map of Europe.

The CD-ROM Guide to Rarer British Birds is designed to run in Internet Explorer or any other modern Web browser on your PC. It includes plenty of photos and video clips, but is not intended as a multimedia leisure title so much as a reference work for those interested in the identification, status, distribution and stories behind Britain's rarest species.

DVDs for children

DVD-Video titles aimed at children show how the real value of DVD lies in the extra fun material and games packed on each disc – all of which can be played on your PC.

Back in 2000, the movie industry was wondering if DVD-Video would ever really take off. The following year it did precisely that – and in a huge way. Reasons for the sudden boom included the falling price of DVD-players and the realisation that Sony's popular games console, the PlayStation 2, could play DVD-Video titles too. However, you don't have to own either in order to be part of the DVD in-crowd because practically all modern PCs come with a fully video-compatible DVD-ROM drive as standard.

This feature comes into its own when playing the special content that is invariably included on a DVD in addition to the main feature film. There is an increasing number of DVDs aimed at children that include Multimedia content which will keep a young audience occupied at a PC,

as well as in front of a TV screen.

One of the best examples is the DVD release of Disney/Pixar's hit movie *Monsters, Inc* which uses computerized 3D animation techniques. This title is packed with extra clips, background information, mini features and games for children. While it makes sense to watch the main movie on a TV set if possible, many people feel more comfortable viewing and playing with the Multimedia extras on their PC.

● Fun extras

The bonus material on the *Monsters, Inc* DVD begins with three additional short films, including *Mike's New Car*, which was created specially for the DVD. Younger children will

Mike's New Car is a short film created specially for the home video and DVD release of Monsters, Inc, featuring main characters Sully and Mike in a new mini-adventure.

appreciate another special item on the disc, *Boo's Door Game*. This is where DVD really comes into its own, because it offers genuine Multimedia entertainment in the form of an interactive game, rather than just another preset video sequence.

The aim of the game is to hunt six missing pieces of Boo's closet door so that big blue Sully can revisit his little human friend. It's quite basic but will appeal particularly to 4 to 7 year olds who will enjoy the simple challenge and bright colours.

More early learning fun can be found in another *Monsters, Inc* Multimedia program, *Welcome to Metropolis*. This recounts the central storyline of the feature film as a child's picture book with cartoon-style artwork and large text for the child to follow. Each page hides additional animations and

MENU SELECTION

The sheer volume of content on a DVD-Video title requires some serious navigation. To help you, DVDs provide simple menu screens, often animated and enhanced with background music in classic Multimedia fashion. You make menu choices and selections on your TV using a remote control handset, or even

more easily on your PC by clicking on them with the mouse. This way, every element of the DVD – from individual scenes to subtitle options – is just a couple of clicks away. Items such as mini features, games and production notes are usually found in an area, or separate disc, entitled 'Bonus Material' or 'Extras'.

The main menu screen will tell you what extras are on the disc apart from the feature film itself. Monsters, Inc (far left) takes a straightforward approach while the DVD interface for Jimmy Neutron – Boy Genius is designed to look like one of Jimmy's gadgets.

Included on the Jimmy Neutron DVD is a documentary which demonstrates how the sketches were transformed into roughs and 3D models, and finally into the fully rendered movie (above and right).

clickable items to discover. If you get lost, characters from the story provide help and guidance.

The *Monsters, Inc* DVD also offers an interesting Abandoned Concepts area. This shows complete animated sequences, but hand-drawn on paper like a moving storyboard. It can be entertaining to pick out scenes, script excerpts and some of the one-liners that made it to the final film.

In addition, the dedicated *Monsters, Inc* fan should take a look at the bonus material provided with the Collector's Edition DVD. By adding a second disc, Pixar has squeezed in even more comedy shorts and features, including some spoof documentaries about Monstropolis and the scream factory.

● Production secrets
Many DVD titles include film-buff items such as a running commentary from the director, filmographies of the actors and so on. The DVD release of the 3D animated movie *Ice Age* – a competitor to *Monsters, Inc* at the time they were in the cinema – includes no less than 14 documentaries explaining

how the film was made, plus a behind-the-scenes programme that was shown on TV. Also crammed on to the disc is a multitude of snippets showing all the animation ever created using the *Ice Age* characters, including movie trailers, deleted scenes and extra shorts.

One clever item on the *Ice Age* DVD is the Animation Progression. This shows you the hand-drawn storyboard, the original 3D layout, unrendered animation and the final movie at the same time. You can switch views using your DVD player's controls or reduce them so they all fit together on the same screen.

If you insert a DVD into your PC you'll discover a multitude of hidden surprises waiting for you.

● The inclusion of extras
A similar approach to fun extras is found in the DVD release of another 3D animated movie for children,

Jimmy Neutron – Boy Genius. This comes with a comprehensive documentary on the making of the film, where children can learn about the process of taking an animated film from a series of drawings to the seamless presentation they can watch at the cinema.

Also included on the DVD are *Jimmy Neutron* cartoon shorts and a five-part cliffhanger serial. Further kids' appeal is guaranteed by the inclusion of two pop videos from the movie soundtrack, featuring Aaron Carter and No Secrets.

● More than a movie
All of the DVDs featured here include plenty of extra material to keep you and any younger viewers in your family entertained. With so much to experiment and play with, including a number of hidden surprises, *Monsters, Inc, Ice Age* and *Jimmy Neutron – Boy Genius* are the kind of DVD titles that may well spend more time in your PC than on your TV.

There's much more to Ice Age than simply light-hearted entertainment. Children will learn all about the true-life archaeological background to the creatures in the film.

CONTACT POINTS

Monsters, Inc DVD
Price: £16.99*
Monsters, Inc Collector's Edition DVD
Price: £21.99*
Walt Disney Home Video
www.disney.co.uk

Ice Age DVD
Price: £19.99*
20th Century Fox
www.iceagemovie.com

Jimmy Neutron – Boy Genius DVD
Price: £19.99*
Paramount Home Entertainment
www.jimmyneutron.com

*UK prices

The Internet

Powerful new ways to search the Web

It's getting easier to find what you want on the Internet. Search engines and other search tools are becoming more sophisticated but simpler to use. Many search sites also offer a range of other features.

As with so much of the Internet, the development of search engines and other ways of accessing the Web's contents moves on apace. Don't be surprised if sites disappear or seem out of date – sites come and go, or are updated, according to popularity and available investment. In Stage 2, pages 138–141, we looked at ordinary search-engine sites, but there are also a number of useful sites that can search through several engines at once, and utility software that offers much the same thing.

Many search sites offer more than just a search facility, hoping that you will use them as your home page, which you would then access every

Powerful new search techniques make finding information on the Web less of a chore.

WHAT IT MEANS

PORTALS

The most useful portals tend to be those that can be customized, allowing you to specify precisely what you want to see when you access them: world news, stock prices, sports updates and so on, although you might well have to specify that you want UK, rather than US content. Portals might also offer access to their own search engine, plus added incentives, such as free email and chat. As such, these are prime candidates for your home page.

time you start surfing. Your home page is, in effect, your launch pad for the rest of the Web.

● **Valuable visitors**
Driving this development is the desire of corporations to be at the heart of the Internet and to own the most frequently visited sites. There are two reasons for this interest: first, the revenue gained from advertising, and second, the long-term prize of sites establishing themselves as leaders, then cashing in on the vast riches the Internet can generate.

So whereas search engines used just to search, they may now offer content – news, features and reviews are common – and personalized pages with customized links, free email, chat and shopping may also be on offer.

In fact, the aim is not just to make you use their search engine as your starting point, but to make it the hub: the place that you always visit, no matter what kind of information you're after. These jazzed-up sites are known as portals, and aim to be your gateway to the Internet.

Here, we cover the big portals, which are mainly based around leading search engines. If you prefer one portal's approach in particular, you might want to make it your home page (see Specifying your home page box, opposite).

The number of visits, or hits, boasted by certain pages can be misleading. For instance, the Netscape and Microsoft sites have a high number of hits because these are the default home-page settings for their respective browsers, and many people don't realize that they can change their home page. It is therefore hard to ascertain how often sites are actually used by surfers.

● **The megasearchers**
Another reason why search engines are diversifying is the proliferation of multiple search sites. These so-called metasearchers and megasearchers access a number of search engines from a single site and use the search services without calling up the sites. A metasearcher accesses engines simultaneously while a megasearcher looks at one engine at a time.

The usual listings-based portals also now have competition. Another type known as a 'crawler' uses an automated piece of software, often called a 'spider', to go hunting for new and updated sites on its own. Crawler-based search sites tend not to offer site links in organised listings, but they can turn up unusual Web sites which would not normally be listed or even checked out by a standard portal.

Engines and portals

Many sites with search engines are also offering customizable content.

Yahoo!
www.yahoo.co.uk

Yahoo! is the classic category-based search engine (or 'directory'). It has been around almost since the start of the Web, has millions of users worldwide, and is one of the most valuable net businesses. From its US origins, it has expanded to cover virtually every country and region in the world. Logging on to Yahoo.co.uk will give you focused news, products and services for the UK – while the same goes for its counterparts in France, Germany, Italy and many other places. It's fast, powerful and offers plenty of extras, such as free email, chat rooms and a customizable My Yahoo! page, tailoring information to whatever you find most useful.

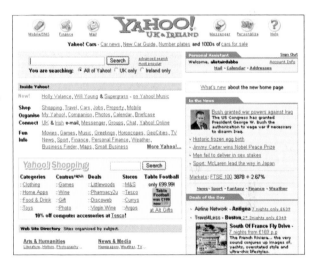

Google
www.google.co.uk

Overtaking the rest of the field at an astounding rate, Google has grown from obscurity to being one of the world's favourite search engines. Appreciated for its simplicity, speed and lack of advertisements, Google is more versatile than it first looks. It can hunt down pictures, check your spelling, translate foreign language pages and integrate stock quotes. Its free Google Toolbar utility for Web browsers is particularly popular.

MSN
www.msn.co.uk

This section of the Microsoft site is the default home page for users of Microsoft's Internet Explorer. It offers the usual features, but is set apart by the quality of the material and its local focus. Rather than giving UK subscribers the score between the Yankees and the Dodgers, for example, it tells you what's happening at Wimbledon or Lords, provides a UK weather forecast and has an excellent mix of national, international and local news. The opening page is continually updated so you'll be able to find all the latest reports and breaking news.

Netscape Search

search.netscape.com

In the same way that the default search engine site for Microsoft Internet Explorer is MSN, the site which appears when you click on the Search button in Netscape Navigator's toolbar is Netscape Search. It's clean and simple, and is styled along the lines of Google – in fact it's really just a Netscape-branded page that accesses Google's core search engine in the background. The one-click access makes it more convenient than Google for many Netscape users, although there are links to other search engines if you prefer to use another one. If you'd like the wider capabilities of a heavyweight portal, visit Netscape's customizable home page instead at www.netscape.com and click on My Netscape.

LookSmart

www.looksmart.co.uk

LookSmart is essentially a business-to-business operation, licensing its Web search database to other portals and Internet-based businesses. You can, however, go to its own site and use the service for free. The directory is maintained by human input with people submitting site reviews for inclusion in the listings. Commercial sites can pay to be listed more prominently but that doesn't mean you can't submit your own personal Web site to the database. Non-commercial sites are listed as a matter of course on LookSmart's Zeal site, and these are integrated back into the main search engine so you can hunt through all sites from one place.

Metasearchers and crawlers

At some sites you can search the search engines. These sites contain metasearchers – searchers that quiz a number of search engines simultaneously and pull together the results. There are also crawlers that roam the Web looking for new sites.

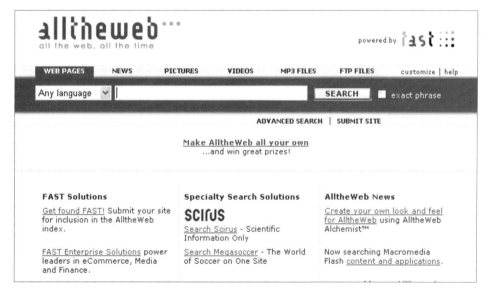

AlltheWeb

www.alltheweb.com

Although primarily a showcase for search engine technology developed by FAST, AlltheWeb is one of the most valuable sites for expert searchers. It lets you hunt for pictures, videos and MP3 audio files as well as news and information pages, all from one page. Quite simply, if you can't find what you are looking for through your favourite search engine, AlltheWeb should be the next stop on your list of search engines. In fact, many users visit AlltheWeb before anything else.

AltaVista
www.altavista.co.uk

AltaVista is a search engine that has reinvented itself by becoming a one-stop portal. It provides both news headlines and links to all sorts of services and information categories. If you simply use the search engine you'll find it fast and thorough, giving accurate and comprehensive results. You can also search for particular types of files, such as music or photographs.

One of AltaVista's most useful features is its translation page, which is accessed by clicking on the Translate link on the main page. If you find an interesting looking site that's written in another language, try using this page to get an instant translation. It's all done by computer – so some nuances and colloquialisms are missed – but the results often tell you what you need to know.

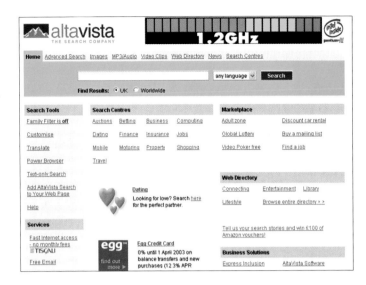

Ask Jeeves
www.askjeeves.co.uk

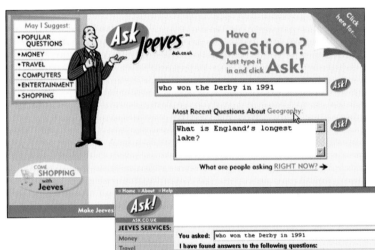

This is something of a two-gimmick search engine. First, it uses the character of Bertie Wooster's famous butler as your guide to all knowledge. Second, it offers to give answers to 'natural language' questions – those put in plain English, interrogative format, such as 'Who won the Derby in 1991?' The answers are not always quite as simple as the questions, as you can see in the screens printed here; to find out that particular horse's name you'll have to do some more searching on the material Jeeves comes up with. In fact, Ask Jeeves isn't really so much of a search engine as a way of submitting searches to a number of other search engines, which then supply the information. As such, it is likely that you'll find what you're after in the end, but you may find it necessary to delve deep into the answers it provides.

Lycos
www.lycos.co.uk

Like Yahoo, Lycos is one of the Web's original search engines, and it even claims to be the originator of the crawling spider concept of automated Internet site mapping. More recently, Lycos threw itself into the business of providing a powerful portal, and now licences its basic site database for everyday searches from FAST. For many people, this actually makes Lycos even more useful, because it also incorporates results from the Open Directory listing compiled by humans, along with a large number of other Web functions and information services. A nice touch is the way Lycos provides alternative suggestions related to your original keyword or search topic underneath each search result.

Smoother Web browsing

Searching for information or a specific site on the World Wide Web often seems like a struggle. We show you how error messages and registration forms are not always the dead ends they seem.

Imagine an ideal Web-browsing world, where you would enter the name of a Web site, press [Enter] and always go straight to the site. We don't live in an ideal world, however, and as you explore the Web you'll encounter a range of browsing obstacles, including error messages, alerts that a 'site has not been found', access restrictions and suggestions that you subscribe to a site. In the next few pages, we show you some common browsing obstacles and how to overcome them.

● Registration form

As you browse the Web, you'll come across requests to register with a site. In many cases, you can gain access to the site by filling in an on-screen form with your name, address and a few personal details. The company running the site asks for the details so that they can compile a profile of the type of visitor to the site. This information is used to persuade advertisers to promote their products on the Web site.

For other Web sites, such as those providing real-time share prices or business services (online company searches, for example), you may need to pay a subscription or enter your credit card details before you can access the site. On the following pages, you will see how to register for *Loot*'s classified advertising site.

It contains thousands of adverts for all sorts of goods from cars to flats – and it's free to register.

● Bells and whistles

Many Web sites use sophisticated techniques that provide video, sound and animation. Don't worry if your browser doesn't have the latest software needed to view and hear the Multimedia effects – downloading and installing plug-ins is easy, as we show on page 141. The plug-ins will enable your browser to show these new features.

● Top two browsers

There are two main Internet browsers – Microsoft's Internet Explorer and Netscape's Communicator/ Navigator – and each has different features. If you have access to both browsers, you will notice that they sometimes display the same Web page in a slightly different way. For example, you may find that text and pictures sometimes line up differently on the screen. However, this is only a matter of concern to the purists and the content is generally the same.

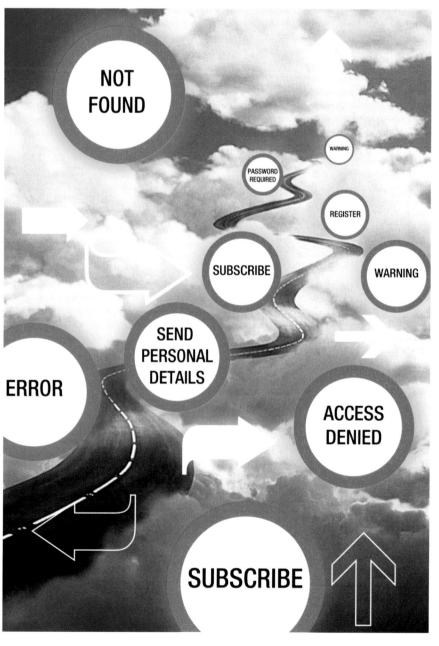

HOW A BROWSER WORKS

A browser works by interpreting the special programming codes that are used to create a page. These codes – called HTML (see Stage 2, page 134) – describe the way that a page is set out, the format of the text and other aspects of the presentation.

● Browser developments

The browser developers are always working on techniques to improve the way information is presented on screen. Problems arise because the latest additions to one browser might not be used by another. So, if a Web site designer wants to use new extensions to the HTML codes developed by Microsoft (see How a brower works box, above), then these can often only be seen if you view the Web site with the latest Microsoft Explorer browser. If you use the Netscape browser (or even an older version of Explorer), the Web page will not look as it is intended.

● Security and warnings

Security on the Internet is essential to protect your personal details. When you move around a site, you are not sending any sensitive information – you are only using your browser to view and jump from page to page. However, many sites ask you to type in information such as your name and other personal details. In such cases, you are sending details about yourself over the Net to another computer.

Both the Microsoft and Netscape Web browsers will warn you when you are about to send personal information. Sometimes this warning is not necessary. If you type a word into a search engine, for example, this isn't sensitive information and there is no problem. In other circumstances, however, you might not appreciate the consequences of sending your credit card or other personal details across the Internet, so your computer reminds you to be cautious.

● Error messages

While browsing the Web, you might also encounter an array of warning messages. Any messages containing a warning triangle will usually have an explanation of the problem your

Just like the roads, the Internet can come to a halt due to heavy traffic. If the Web site you are trying to visit is congested, your browser will suggest you visit it later.

Here are two error messages that you might encounter on the Web – one indicating that the Web browser has been unable to access your chosen Web site without giving a reason (bottom), the other suggesting that you have typed an incorrect Web address into your browser (top).

browser is experiencing. It might be asking you to confirm your request to open a file over the Internet or it might be telling you it was unable to download a file you requested.

Some of the most common error messages are those which announce that a Web site you want to visit is busy and that you should try again later. This is usually caused by congestion – many other people are trying to visit the site at the same time. You might also encounter warning messages saying that a Web page you have requested does not exist. This happens if the Web site has been updated and old pages have been deleted.

Shopping with security on the Internet

Amazon.com is an Internet success story. This online bookshop has tapped a worldwide market of book-buyers using the Internet.

Retailers don't want potential customers to be scared off by security worries. Amazon.com has addressed this problem so successfully that it now has more than 20 million customers. The company is a well-known and respected retailer that recognized concern over Internet security.

Using a secure server ensures that credit card details are encoded on your PC before being sent to Amazon's computer. Once the details are in their computer, Amazon cannot be accessed from the outside world. If people still don't trust the Internet, Amazon offers other options such as emailing the first half of a credit card number and faxing the rest – or just posting a cheque!

Signing up to a Web site

Don't be afraid of telling the provider of an Internet site a few things about yourself. Here we show you what a simple process it is.

1 Registering with a Web site is easy and is usually free. A good example is *Loot*'s free classified advertising site (www.loot.com). You can browse and search the ads immediately, but to advertise you must first register. Click on the Register link on *Loot*'s home page.

2 On the next page, start by typing in your email address and then select a password (make sure it's not the same as your email password, however).

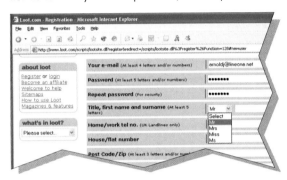

3 The registration form also asks you for some personal details, such as your name, age and occupation. You must fill in all the fields or your registration will not be accepted.

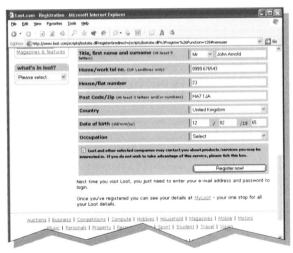

4 Many sites have a tick box that lets you opt out of mailing lists. When you have filled in all the details, click on the Register now! button (inset) to submit the form.

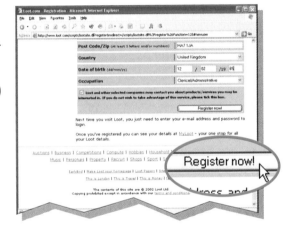

TAKING DOWN YOUR DETAILS

Many Web sites ask you to complete a registration form before you are allowed to use the site. The sites requiring registration may have thousands of pages of information on them. These pages have to be kept up to date and therefore require a lot of work to keep them running efficiently. Information about what kind of people (their age, country and interests, for example) visit the site will help the site attract advertising revenue to pay for this work. Some sites that don't charge visitors, such as Yahoo!, have a multi-million dollar turnover as a result of the advertising that appears on their pages.

5 Now that you have registered, you can place classified ads for free. Go to *Loot*'s home page and click on the Place a free ad link.

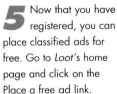

6 You can now use *Loot*'s step-by-step advertising forms. These are stored in your own space on *Loot*'s computers so that you can renew the ad at a later date.

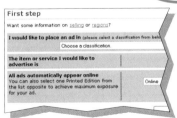

How to add an animation plug-in

Macromedia's Shockwave and Flash players are Web browser plug-ins that will breathe life into pictures and previously blank screens on Web sites. Here we show how to download these plug-ins.

1 When you visit a Web site for the first time, you are often given information about how to view the site at its best. Many sites rely upon the animation and interactive features of the Macromedia Flash plug-in. If you don't already have this common plug-in, a message will appear asking if you want to install it. As Flash is relatively quick to download, it will install itself automatically after the download has finished.

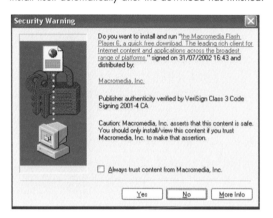

2 A larger download such as Macromedia Shockwave may require you to visit the Macromedia home page (www.macromedia.com) first. Click on the Downloads link and then click on the Macromedia Shockwave Player link. Then click on the Install Now link to begin the download and automated installation procedure. A Security Warning box will check that you do want to download from the Internet.

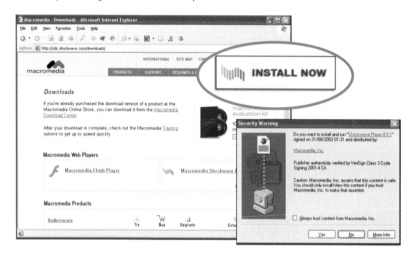

3 Shockwave takes around 5–10 minutes to download with a 56K modem. While it is downloading, you can still browse other Web sites. A little window sits in the background, showing you the progress of the download.

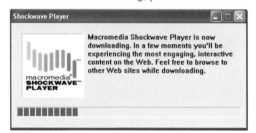

4 Once the download is complete, Shockwave will automatically start its installation routine. You will be prompted to fill in the screen with your details so you can get regular news updates from Macromedia. Click on Next to proceed.

5 The installation only takes a few seconds, during which time your Web browser will exit and then immediately relaunch. A test page at the Macromedia site will open up to demonstrate that Shockwave is now working.

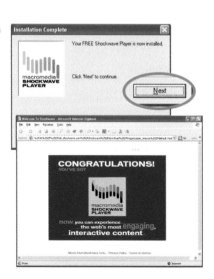

6 Armed with the Shockwave and Flash plug-ins, which work automatically within your Web browser, you can now view the animation and interactive features of any Web site which uses these plug-ins. To experience some of the slickest entertainment on the Web visit www.shockwave.com.

Introducing newsgroups

Where can you get the facts you need to settle a friendly argument? Where should you go when you need professional advice? How can you find new recipes for a dinner party? Newsgroups can provide the answers to all your questions.

You've already seen how to get to grips with two of the Internet's most popular features – email (see Stage 1, pages 150–153) and browsing the World Wide Web (see Stage 2, pages 134–137). But there's another popular part of the Internet that millions of people find just as interesting and useful, and that's newsgroups.

Newsgroups provide a way for you to make contact with people all over the world who share your interests. You can ask for advice, exchange experiences, pool information and even participate in debates.

It's a little like writing and sending email. The difference is that when you write to a newsgroup (known as making a posting), your message is sent to special computers which everybody who participates in the newsgroup can access in order to read what you've written. Then the members can reply if they want – either by posting a comment to your message which can then be viewed by all the newsgroup users, or by sending a private email to you.

● A newsgroup for every interest

There are newsgroups specializing in just about every subject you can imagine. Some are devoted to serious academic debate, while others are for swapping recipes. There are also newsgroups for almost every type of hobby, sport and leisure activity. For example, there are newsgroups for gardening, music, cooking, football, UFOs, TV and cinema and keeping animals as pets – and these are just a few of the thousands of subjects.

It's easy to see what a great resource newsgroups offer and how much fun

it can be to get in touch with like-minded people anywhere in the world. Newsgroups are free to join: all you need is access to the Internet and an Internet newsreader program.

● Joining a newsgroup

If you have an account with an Internet service provider (ISP), you probably already have everything you need to join a newsgroup. Sometimes

the Internet newsreader program is a separate piece of software, but the latest email and Internet browser programs include the facilities needed to access newsgroups. It's simply a matter of taking a few moments to set up your software properly before you try it out (see page 144).

When you send, or post, a message to a newsgroup, it is transmitted to a special computer called a news server. There isn't one big central news server but many scattered all around the world. They are operated by different organizations, such as companies, universities and ISPs. These news servers swap messages frequently, so yours are initially sent to your

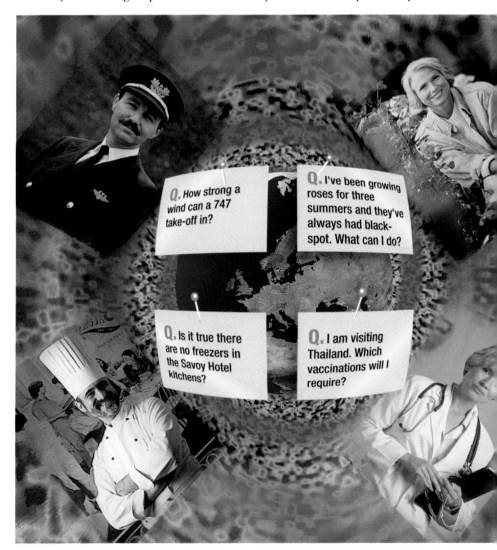

Q. How strong a wind can a 747 take-off in?

Q. I've been growing roses for three summers and they've always had black-spot. What can I do?

Q. Is it true there are no freezers in the Savoy Hotel kitchens?

Q. I am visiting Thailand. Which vaccinations will I require?

local news server and then passed on to all the other news servers across the world.

Know your newsgroups

Each newsgroup covers a particular topic. But newsgroups almost always have cryptic names, so how do you find the right newsgroup for the subject in which you're interested? The first clue usually lies in the newsgroups' strange names. Typically, newsgroup names are made up of

Q. How strong a wind can a 747 take-off in?

several parts, each separated by a full stop. For example, rec.music.beatles is the newsgroup where fans of The Beatles communicate with each other.

As there are so many newsgroups (currently over 40,000, but this number is changing all the time), the Internet community has organized them into a hierarchical structure to keep them manageable. At the top level (the first part of the name), they

are split into broad subject areas. For instance, comp contains computing newsgroups, biz has business newsgroups and, as in the previous example, rec (short for recreation) covers newsgroups for hobbies, interests and leisure activities.

Within each top-level set of newsgroups, you will find subsets. For instance, rec.music is the subset of the main rec heading that contains newsgroups about music. As music itself is such a huge area, you will find many newsgroups within it catering for particular tastes in music. We've already mentioned one example, and others of interest include rec.music.country.western for country music or rec.music.bluenote for jazz fans.

Family concerns

One set of newsgroups you should be aware of – and wary of if you have children who share your computer – are the alt (short for alternative) newsgroups. These often discuss alternative lifestyle and/or adult material in a frank, sometimes explicit fashion (see Alternative choices, below left).

Take your time

Once you have found a newsgroup that seems interesting, the next step is to join it (see page 145). It's a good idea not to wade straight in and start posting messages, however. Read the postings other people make for a while – this will give you an idea of the sorts of things being discussed in the newsgroup. It will also give you guidance on the level of behaviour and politeness other members of the group will expect from you if you join in. Some newsgroups are informal, but others expect certain standards from their members.

When you first join up with a newsgroup, look out for a posting about FAQs (short for Frequently Asked Questions). This is a text file (often just a long message) which will explain the behaviour expected of the newsgroup members, including netiquette, and describe the subjects the newsgroup was set up to discuss. In particular, the

FAQ file will provide you with basic information you might want to know. This will help you to avoid asking questions the newsgroup has answered many times before.

Don't be intimidated

As a final note, some newsgroups can be a bit over-critical of newcomers' mistakes. Don't worry if you are 'told off' by any of the more experienced users. There are some fanatical people who take any breaks in convention or slips in netiquette very seriously. The best thing to do if this takes place is just refuse to be intimidated and use any criticism as a useful learning exercise, which will allow you to get the most out of any newsgroup you choose to join.

Q. I've been growing roses for three summers and they've always had black-spot. What can I do?

Setting up a newsgroup reader

Before you can read and post newsgroup messages, you must first spend a few minutes setting up your newsgroup software to communicate with your Internet service provider's servers and downloading the full list of newsgroups.

1 You don't need to splash out on extra newsgroup software because newsgroups rely on email messages to distribute postings. Windows' own email program, Outlook Express, is perfect for composing and reading newsgroup messages. Click on the E-mail entry near the top of the Start menu.

2 When the program window appears, click on the news entry in the Folders panel on the left of the Outlook Express window. The exact name will vary depending on the ISP you have joined, but it should be at the bottom of the list. If there's no news entry on your computer, see No news? box, below.

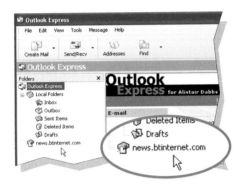

3 If you haven't used newsgroups on your PC before, Outlook Express has nothing to display and it suggests that you start by retrieving a list of newsgroups from the newsgroup server. Click on the Yes button.

4 Next, connect to the Internet when your ISP's dial-up dialog box pops up. When the connection is established, Outlook Express locates the server and starts to download the newsgroup list.

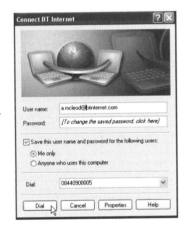

5 Because this is the first time you have connected to your ISP's newsgroup server, there's a lot to download, with over 40,000 newsgroups to choose from. However, at this point Outlook Express is only downloading the names of the newsgroups – not the messages – so the download shouldn't take more than a minute or so.

6 Once the list has fully downloaded, it appears in alphabetical order in the main panel of the Newsgroup Subscriptions dialog box. You're now ready to choose which newsgroups to join (see opposite). Note: if your children share your PC, you should be aware that there are lots of newsgroups that cater for adults, and many have very explicit names. Think about installing a parental control program (see Stage 2, pages 146–149).

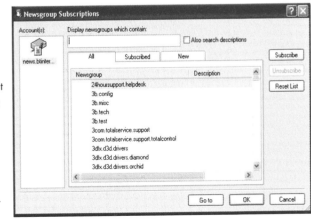

NO NEWS?

Most Internet service providers (ISPs) set up their software so that your PC displays an entry for their own newsgroup servers in the Folders panel (see Step 2). However, some do not, so you may have to set it up manually. To do this, first check your ISP's documentation or Web pages for information about its newsgroup servers. Select Accounts from the Outlook Express Tools menu, click on the Add button in the dialog box and then on News to enter this information.

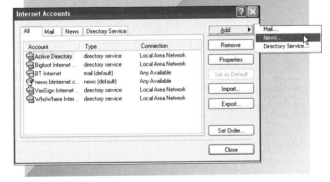

Subscribing to newsgroups and posting messages

There are newsgroups to cover every subject under the sun; once you have subscribed to one, you can read messages and post your own for other people to comment on.

1 Once you have downloaded the list of newsgroups (see opposite), you're ready to subscribe. It takes too long to look through the whole list, so type one of your hobbies into the 'Display newsgroups which contain:' box.

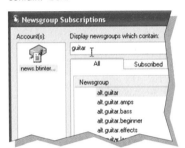

2 Now that the list is much shorter, scroll through and find an interesting sounding newsgroup. Click on it once and then click on the Subscribe button. A small icon appears to show that you have marked it. You can add more subscriptions but, for the moment, it's worth keeping things manageable by starting with just one. Click on the OK button to go back to the main Outlook Express window.

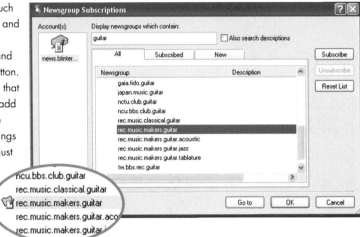

3 To read messages posted to your newsgroup, select your newsgroup, click on the Settings button and select New Messages Only. Then click on the Synchronize Account button.

4 Outlook Express then downloads the newsgroup messages and displays them. Click on the newsgroup in the Folders panel on the left and the right-hand part of the window changes: message titles appear in the top panel, with the text of the highlighted message in the panel below. Click on any message to read it.

5 When you see a message you want to respond to, click on the Reply Group button on the Outlook Express toolbar. Use the message window to type in a reply just as you would type a reply to a normal email message. Click on the Send button when you've finished.

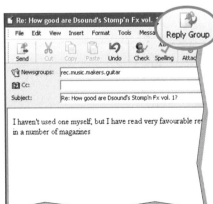

6 To start a completely new topic, click on the New Post button instead. This pops up a similar message window. Type your message in the same way, but this time, remember to give the message a clear subject – this is vital in busy newsgroups where your message may be easily overlooked.

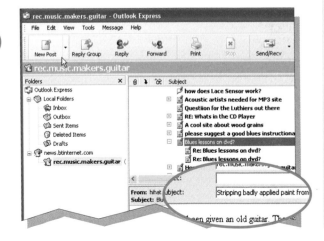

PC TIPS

When you first subscribe to a newsgroup, there may be several thousand messages to download. This can take time, but it's a good idea to browse through these messages to get a feel for newsgroup netiquette – which can vary from newsgroup to newsgroup – before posting your own questions. Taking a look first will give you confidence that you're asking the right audience.

Climate change

The dramatic changes in both weather and climate that the world has experienced in recent years have made this subject an important global issue. Today there are many sites on the web which deal with this serious topic.

R ecent years have put climate at the forefront of global concerns. The devastation caused by Hurricane Mitch in Central America in 1998 was one of the most horrifying examples of what the weather can do. It is now thought that the climate is in the process of changing and that in the future events like Mitch might become more common.

Elsewhere, but particularly in North and South America, there have been droughts, deluges, heatwaves and great freezes that have caused enormous damage to people and property. Devastating floods in Prague caused mass destruction in August 2002 and even Britain felt the damaging effects of the weather when a tornado hit north-west England at the start of 2002. These examples of 'extreme' or 'severe' weather back up the climatologists' arguments that weather systems are changing and we need to take firm steps on a global basis to counter them.

Dramatic changes in the weather worldwide are a symptom of climatic change. The old certainties can no longer be relied upon and global warming may be responsible for shifting the familiar climate zones across the planet.

● Global warming

There are plenty of Internet sites with information on the dramatic weather events that are taking place. While there is occasionally a ghoulish side to some of these sites, most present the awesome effects of climate alongside serious debate.

The main cause for concern is, of course, global warming. The steady rise in temperatures during this century, largely caused by increased carbon dioxide emissions leading to the 'greenhouse effect', is widely accepted to be the underlying cause of much of our extreme weather. Many sites deal with global warming, approaching the subject from its various perspectives.

● Propaganda sites

Educational sites aim to present a clear explanation of the global warming phenomenon that will make sense to the general public.

In general, these sites do the job very well, using diagrams, animations and clear text explanations to get the main points across. However, they may also have what might be called a 'propaganda' purpose: they want to stimulate public demand for more stringent and effective measures to manage global warming. One reason for this is that, despite a series of inter-governmental meetings over the past few years, in which the nations of the world attempted to reach an agreement on just how carbon dioxide emissions could be managed, there are still some countries that are rather reluctant to take the required action.

● Politics and environment

You can find plenty of Internet sites that analyse the agreements made at Buenos Aires and later at Kyoto, and outline the progress – or lack of it – since. These sites can be heavy going, as this is a political issue as well as an environmental one. However, if you make the effort, you'll find yourself well informed on just what we, the human race, are doing about these major changes to our planet.

While everyone now agrees that global warming is taking place, there are different opinions on how we should deal with it. On one side are those who argue for 'mitigation', believing that we should cut emissions and try to halt, or even reverse, the trend. On the other side are those who argue that we should go for 'adaptation', and learn to live with global warming, taking appropriate measures, such as limiting water use. Both sides of the argument are well presented on the Internet.

Scientists would never have been able to come to any firm conclusions about global warming (or other climatic changes) without a mass of historical climatic data to work on. Much of this data can also be found on the Internet, and the facts are often very impressive even if the presentation could be improved.

You'll find a wealth of data on the Web for the world's hottest, coldest, wettest or driest places – so whether you are planning a trip or researching a project, the Internet is bound to provide the information you need.

Action on climate change

Browsing the Internet will give you some useful background information on climate change or, if you want more detail, there are many sites that deal specifically with this subject. Some of the best are featured here.

United Nations Environment Programme

www.unep.ch/conventions

The UN is at the forefront of just about every initiative on global climate change and the environmental disasters it has caused. Here, you can find out about its various programmes, such as the Convention on Climate Change, the Convention on Biological Diversity, and the Convention to Combat Desertification. It's all very clearly presented, both on screen and in downloadable .pdf files, which you can study offline at your leisure.

Climate Change Campaign

www.panda.org/climate

This sub-section of the Worldwide Fund for Nature site is both an education and a call for action. It presents a clear and elegant interface that makes it easy for you to get straight to the information you want. Don't worry if you feel ignorant about the subject, the home page provides useful information on the problems and causes of climate change. Elsewhere on the site there is a comprehensive and constantly changing round-up of global news related to climate change – thankfully not all of it is bad. The impact on ecosystems and individual species is also presented clearly and powerfully.

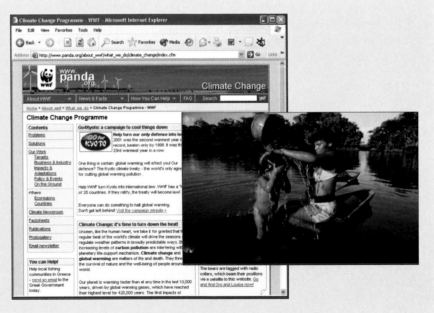

The Ozone Hole Tour

www.atm.ch.cam.ac.uk/tour

Created by the Centre for Atmospheric Science at the University of Cambridge, this site is an object lesson in how to present the results of a scientific study to the general public in an easy-to-understand way. With a host of Multimedia aids, it tells the story of the discovery of the ozone hole in Antarctica and the continuing research into it. There's a lot of detail, but the subject is explained with great clarity.

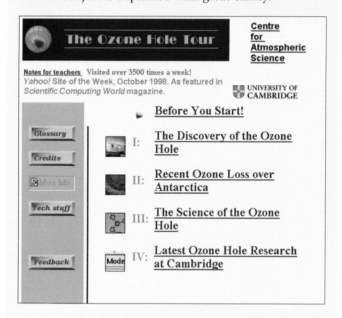

Death Valley

http://deathvalley.areaparks.com

Death Valley in California is one of the hottest spots on Earth (see the World Temperature Extremes site at www.iinet.net.au/~jacob/worldtp.html for temperatures) and, as such, this largely tourist-orientated site gives excellent advice on how to cope with the heat for those driving, walking or participating in any of the many activities available in the vicinity. It's well worth looking at if you're thinking of visiting the valley.

American Petroleum Institute

www.api.org/globalclimate

If you want to hear a dissenting voice on global warming, this is one of the few sites to present it clearly. The US oil companies don't agree with the current prognosis or cures for global warming. Their case is presented without hysteria, and includes lots of material about what they have done for the US public. Good links to sites that present opposing views are also provided.

WorldClimate

www.worldclimate.com

This site provides the data that climatologists use to identify whether any long-term patterns in climate change are emerging. More than 85,000 records give you an idea of what the weather is normally like, using average temperatures rather than extremes. Just type in the name of a place and the site will find the relevant data. The amount of information provided varies from place to place, but may include the average temperature and data on rainfall and sea-level pressure.

National Oceanic and Atmospheric Administration

www.noaa.gov

The NOAA is the USA's top climatic and weather research body, and has a rich Web site. It contains sub-sections that are worthwhile sites in their own right. You can get access to statistics and research from NESDIS – the National Environmental Satellite, Data and Information Service – and there are fascinating 3D diagrams showing visualizations of live climate phenomena one click away from the main page.

Weather Land

www.weatherland.com

A one-man site that, despite its limited resource, crams in a lot of weather and climate-related material in an attractive package. There's a great deal of material on the latest storms and hurricanes, a separate hurricane page and a special El Niño page. Perhaps the most attractive element is the live Web cams page, which features a range of sites as diverse as the Wailing Wall in Jerusalem and New York City, so you can check the latest climatic conditions for countries throughout the world.

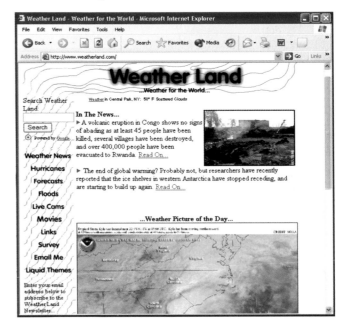

El Niño and La Niña

Many believe El Niño and La Niña are responsible for a wide variety of disastrous weather events in recent years. This Web site explains why.

www.cdc.noaa.gov/ENSO

El Niño causes disruption of ocean-atmospheric patterns in the Pacific Ocean and is thought to be responsible for a wide variety of disastrous weather events in recent years. The El Niño page provides just about the best introduction you'll find on the Web to this strange phenomenon. There are excellent explanations of what El Niño is, together with colourful diagrams and maps, and there's even an animation that you can watch.

The NOAA (National Oceanic and Atmospheric Administration) does a similarly successful job on the La Niña phenomenon – which is comparable to El Niño, but is characterized by cold, rather than warm, ocean temperatures. This site tells you masses of fascinating details about these forces and it also provides excellent links to other sources of information.

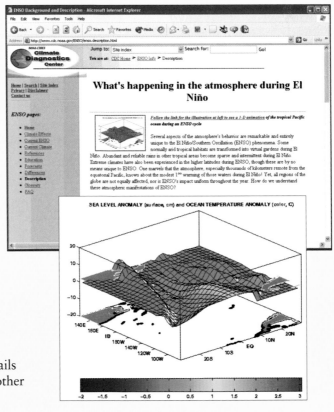

Online shopping

Internet shopping has evolved rapidly in its brief lifespan as traditional retailers have moved from 'bricks to clicks' to challenge the Web's innovators.

In the beginning of online shopping were the innovators, such as Amazon (www.amazon.co.uk), online sellers of books originally but now selling CDs, videos, and just about everything else. From a standing start, such outfits grew incredibly fast, using the vast amounts of venture capital they had raised to launch sites in all major world languages and to offer tempting discounts on many items.

The first companies on the Web also developed the new technologies, techniques and systems that make online shopping work for the consumer: easy registration, virtual shopping carts, safe transmission of credit card data and prompt home delivery of the physical item.

Traditional retailers were at first left behind, but it has not taken them long to catch up, and they are now beginning to dominate the online shopping universe. This is clearest in the field of groceries, where Britain's supermarkets have invested heavily in Web sites for home shopping, along with the delivery services to get your goods to you. In fact Tesco, while continuing to invest in its traditional stores, has claimed to be the world's largest online grocery service.

Buying your groceries online is a very attractive proposition for many of us but, before you rush to log on and order the baked beans and kitchen roll, you must check that your area is covered by the service. Such online services always begin in the heavily populated urban areas before spreading out to the regions and countryside. All of the

If going to the shops drives you mad, try Internet shopping and you'll never have to walk the supermarket's aisles again. With secure means of ordering and paying, there's nothing to stop you going virtual shopping.

supermarket Web sites have 'postcode checkers' so you can find out in a click if they can deliver to you.

Catalogue companies seem an even better fit with the Internet than supermarkets. They have found real advantages on the Web – as access to the Internet increases, fewer costly catalogues will need to be printed and mailed. In addition, the Web allows catalogue retailers to alter stock and prices almost instantly. Catalogue companies in the UK already have a strong Internet presence, and other European retailers are joining in.

At the same time, high street fashion and clothing companies are also building Web sites that have something of a catalogue feel, as in the cases of Top Shop and Marks & Spencer (see page 152).

● Techno beats
New technology implies radical change in both what and how we buy. This is particularly true wherever a

SECURITY

The security of any financial details you divulge online has been a major concern since the early days of the Internet, and this is still the case today. All reputable online shopping sites use powerful data encryption techniques to scramble your data, and will make it clear on their home page that they do so; if there is no statement about security, then steer clear of the site.

While encryption does not guarantee absolute safety, it is pretty effective, and makes online shopping no more dangerous than giving your card number to a salesperson over the telephone. What encryption cannot do, however, is insure against human error; most of the notorious breaches of Internet security have occurred where someone made the mistake of putting a secret file (with customer names, addresses and credit card details) in an unprotected area of a Web site, where anyone could stumble across it.

product can be delivered digitally. For example, with shareware all you have to do is log on to a Web site, give credit card details and download a program straight to your hard disk. It is also possible to buy music online – the digital MP3 format (see MP3 sites, right) allows consumers to download an almost CD-quality song in only a few minutes, which has led to a boom in sites that (illegally) sell performers' work or let fans swap audio files.

● Is the price right?

Checking who has the best deal on an item can be a time-consuming chore. But a relatively new breed of site promises to take the legwork out of online shopping. You simply type in the item you want and the site's software gets to work, trawling the online retailers and reporting back with sites and price comparisons (see page 152).

MP3 SITES

MP3 stands for MPEG Layer-3, a compression technique that can reduce a CD music file to half its previous size. Because the resulting files are smaller, they are ideal for sending over the Internet. Despite court action in the US against some sites offering MP3 files, there are still plenty of legal sites around.

For example, iCrunch (www.icrunch.com) offers a huge range of tunes from independent labels at 99p per download. You can preview tunes online and then buy one at a time or get a collection. And there's plenty of additional content, such as a beginner's guide and label profiles, to give the site more depth. BeSonic (www.besonic.com) isn't really involved in online shopping. Rather, it's more of a showcase site where unsigned artists in pretty much every genre of popular music can display their wares. Downloads are free in return for your email address, which is used to compile the download charts.

Shopping lists

Some are born to shop, others tag along behind looking bored. But, with online shopping, you can shop from the comfort of your home.

Haburi
www.haburi.com

If you want designer clothes and accessories without paying designer prices, take a look at the Haburi Web site. This site works like an international factory outlet store: it offers a mix of designer brands with typical discounts of 25% to 60%. There are even greater savings to be had on the Bargain Basement pages. If you're worried that you may be tempted to spend more than you can afford, you can use the price range filter to ensure that the high-ticket items are safely hidden from view. To get a fashion edge over your friends, join Club Haburi and receive advance notice of special offers and a personalized Haburi shopping page. As you'd expect with online shopping, the site offers a good returns policy and free shipping once you're spending £60 or more.

La Redoute
www.redoute.co.uk

Mounting a stylish French challenge to the UK's traditional catalogue powerhouses is La Redoute. Its online store is well stocked with clothes for all members of the family. Special discounts and prices are also featured on the site, and the ranges are smart and tempting throughout, whether moderately priced or from designers such as Laura Clément. Delivery takes 5–10 days and costs £2.95, no matter how many items are ordered. And – as should be the case for all clothing sites – any returns are free.

Marks & Spencer

www.marksandspencer.com

Just as they have jazzed up their high street stores, so M&S have revamped their Web site to make for a more pleasing shopping experience. There's a good range of clothing on view for men, women and children. A particularly good point is that all images are enlargeable, so you can see exactly what you'll get. Delivery is promised in 48 hours for a £2.95 fee and all returns are free of postage (or you can take them to your nearest store). They'll also give you a full no-quibble refund.

TopShop

www.tops.co.uk

Popular with both the young follower of fashion on a budget and the celebrities who like to mix the designer look with high street styles, the TopShop empire just seems to get bigger and better – so much so that the flagship store at Oxford Circus is now the world's largest fashion store. This site is clearly laid out and simple to use, although it has a much more limited range of collections than the store itself offers. You can check out the new arrivals which are updated weekly, look at the measurements for the tall and petite collections, read up on fashion advice, find out about events at the Oxford Circus store and, most importantly, purchase any of the clothes featured.

Price comparison

Just key in the name or type of product and 'intelligent' software will scour the Web, reporting back instantly on who is charging what, where and for how much.

ShopSmart

uk.shopsmart.com

One of the longer established and higher profile UK sites, it compares the prices of books, videos, CDs, computer games and consumer electronic items so you can quickly find the site offering the cheapest deal. However, ShopSmart offers more than just comparison – it also lists and rates hundreds of online stores in a wide range of categories. The comments are intelligent and far from uncritical, and browsing the site will inevitably throw up dozens of Internet stores you'll want to visit.

Kelkoo

www.kelkoo.co.uk

Like Shopsmart, this site also aims to offer both a shopping guide and price comparisons. The comparisons extend to include computers, hi-fi, household goods and garden furniture, along with the other usual categories. As these sites mature they will be able to offer increasingly more serious and credible price comparisons on a huge range of goods and services. At the moment, they're limited in scope, but still very much worth using; you could save as much as £5 on a single hardback book.

Supermarket sweep

After initial scepticism, the supermarkets have embraced online shopping in a big way, selling not just groceries but a wide range of other goods, too.

Tesco

www.tesco.com

Tesco offers the online shopper a vast range of goods in addition to its grocery range. You can buy books, videos, electrical equipment and even financial products. The site is colourful and easy to navigate, and although there is a lengthy registration process, it does make return visits much quicker and easier. Delivery costs between £3.99 and £6.49 and there's a wide range of time slots to choose from, up to 10pm on weekdays.

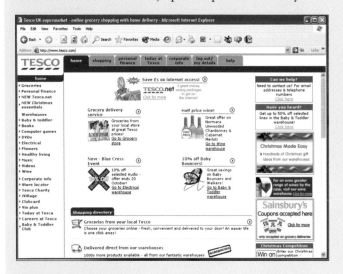

Asda@thome

www.asda.co.uk

Once you have registered, which involves giving your postcode (to check that Asda deliver to your area) and choosing a PIN, you can browse through the store's virtual aisles or search for particular items. The site contains very few graphics, which makes online shopping a quick, if rather uninspiring, affair.

Waitrose Direct

www.waitrose.com

Not only does this site enable you to do all of your grocery shopping online, but it also provides numerous food and cocktail recipes, as well as other services such as Waitrose flower delivery and Web access. You can also use the site to find a restaurant, or even book a holiday thanks to the combined efforts of Waitrose and British Airways.

The Sainsbury's To You site

www.sainsburystoyou.com

This well-designed Web site is quick to load and easy to use. There's a straightforward postcode check to see if you live in an appropriate area for delivery. If you don't have time to browse the extensively stocked virtual aisles, you can use 'your usual' – a list of products compiled for you based on what you have ordered from the site previously. And you can book a delivery slot up to three weeks in advance.

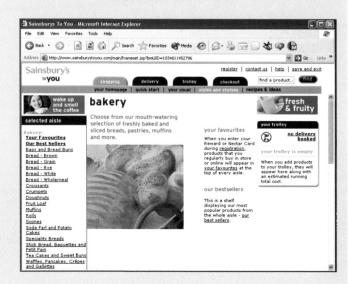

Antiques and collectibles

The current interest in antiques, collectibles and treasured 'junk' is phenomenal – and the Internet hasn't been slow to promote or exploit it.

Ever since the UK television show *Going for a Song* made a star out of the elderly antiquarian Arthur Negus, antiques have been a topic of enduring interest – even for those of us who don't have the necessary financial resources to buy a Meissen figurine or a Chippendale chair. That popularity has been reinforced by other British TV programmes, such as *The Antiques Roadshow* and *Bargain Hunt*, which make us all wonder if we haven't got something of value tucked away in the attic. This widespread interest is, unsurprisingly, strongly reflected on the Internet.

As with many subjects, the Internet offers a range of opportunities with regard to antiques: you can further a practical – perhaps professional – interest by buying and selling online; the casual antiques fancier can broaden his or her knowledge by tapping into the large amounts of

WHAT IS AN ANTIQUE?

There's no hard and fast definition of what an antique is, but it's generally accepted that an object must be over 100 years old to qualify. Even then, however, we need to make allowances. There's a lively trade, for example, in antique or 'classic' wristwatches – and these didn't exist 100 years ago. Very old and rare items dating back many centuries – or even millennia – are known as antiquities. While there's a lot of excellent material about antiques on the Web, there's much less about antiquities, possibly because there are not so many about to buy.

Antiques dealers can provide a global shop window for their stock by using Internet Web sites.

expert information available; and the rest of us can simply indulge our idle curiosity by gazing at the beautiful, strange or simply very expensive objects on view.

● Things to collect

As well as antiques, there's a further category of objects that should be included here – 'collectibles'. These are more modern items, often taken from popular culture and sometimes only a few years old, such as film posters, pop memorabilia, and even spin-off merchandise from the *Wallace and Gromit* animated films. The term refers to anything that people collect since, as soon as a number of people value a certain type of object, you can guarantee that lively trading will follow. Nowadays, an Internet community

can be formed seemingly overnight to support such an interest.

So whether your interest is at the Sotheby's or *Star Wars* end of the market, you'll be well served on the Web. The major international auction houses, such as Sotheby's, all have elegant and authoritative Web sites, offering everything from background material and historical explanation to, of course, exhaustive details of their present, past and forthcoming sales.

Many smaller antique dealers have also set up Web sites which serve as a shop window for their wares. These online catalogues are often an excellent source of information about any given area of antiques, providing detailed descriptions of objects, and

very often photographs as well, which you can simply browse through if you're not interested in buying.

If you want to buy and sell, rather than window-shop, the Internet doesn't disappoint. Online auctions are increasingly popular, giving you the chance to get hold of objects that you might otherwise never have known about, from far-flung lands you would probably never visit. You simply type in your bid and wait to see if you are the winner.

The Web is now so vast and so lively that, whatever the object of your collecting passion, you're sure to find it somewhere, either by using a search engine or by browsing among the antique sites.

Visiting antiques sites

No matter what your level of interest, you can still bid for an Old Master or find a missing Teletubby.

Architectural Heritage

www.architectural-heritage.co.uk

These days it's not just objects but entire buildings – or at least parts of them – that can qualify as antiques. This site sells original and antique garden ornaments, chimney-pieces and panelled rooms for you to buy to create a noble country-house look in your home. Typical items include an English 17th-century oak-panelled room, a stone faun for the garden and a 17th-century limestone chimney-piece. It's a lovely collection of objects, all of which are illustrated; a click expands each picture to give you a better idea of what the item looks like.

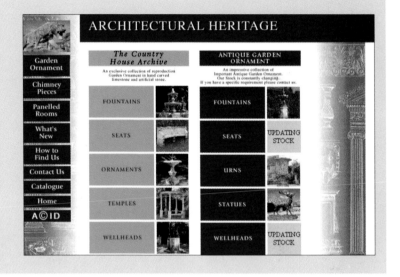

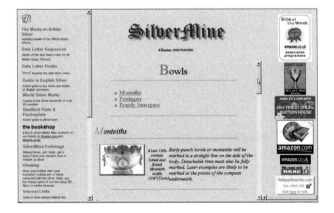

SilverMine

freespace.virgin.net/a.data/

If silver is your fancy, then you really should visit this informative site. At its core is a guide to British silverware, complete with historical overview and notes on the development of styles and forms such as cruets, teapots and so forth. There's a detailed listing of marks from the ten British assay offices, as well as information on silver marks from around the world. There's also an Exchange area, where you can buy, sell, swap, or merely ask questions. All the pictures are in black and white, but that doesn't detract at all from the quality of this site.

Antiqueweb

www.antiqueweb.co.uk

This is an umbrella site, bringing together a number of UK dealers and events under one roof. The main point of interest for the UK antiques fan is its comprehensive listing of antique fairs. Although the site is based in Lancashire and has a good coverage of the north, its listings also provide a comprehensive nationwide resource of what's on where and when.

Antiques World
www.antiquesworld.com

The aim of this site is to put buyers and sellers in touch with each other, and its core is the Marketplace section, which is essentially a Wanted and For Sale classified advertising area. It seems to be very popular and the powerful search engine brings up plenty of good results. The site also features an introduction to antiques and collectibles for those just starting out, as well as an extensive antiques book store in association with Amazon.

ONLINE AUCTIONS

Online auctions take place for all sorts of things, but they're particularly popular in the world of antiques and collectibles. Unlike a real auction, you don't bid against others in real time; instead, you examine the lot (which, of course, is not exactly foolproof), and then submit whatever you think is an appropriate bid.

On some sites – such as eBay – you can use a facility known as 'proxy bidding', whereby you submit the maximum price you're willing to pay and the increments by which your bid may increase; the software then ups your bid if others put in a higher one, until you reach your limit.

Auctions are exciting ways to buy, but they can also be dangerous, because it's easy to get carried away. It's wise to check out the site to assure yourself of its trustworthiness, and it might be worth emailing a request for testimonials. Also, remember that a bid at auction is a 'binding and irrevocable offer to purchase': if your bid wins, you have to go through with it.

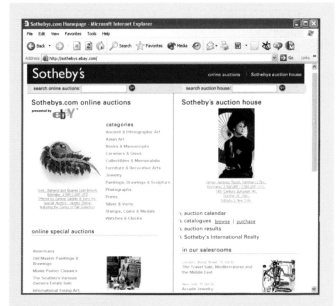

Sotheby's
www.sothebys.com

This is a predictably impressive and suave site with a wide variety of online auctions of classy art and antiques. These are backed up by expert articles on collecting everything from art to stamps, or even unmounted gemstones. The site also has an extensive calendar of Sotheby's auctions around the world so you can always find out where you need to be.

Kool Collectables
www.koolcollectables.com

This UK company specializes in collectibles from popular movies and TV programmes – *Star Trek*, *Star Wars*, *Lord of the Rings* and the *Wallace and Gromit* films, to name but a few. The dolls, toys, walkie talkies and other bizarre spin-off merchandise from such productions have rapidly become sought-after collectors' items. This site offers the ideal opportunity to complete your collection of, for example, *Star Wars* figurines, or simply to find out what the old junk in the toy-chest might be worth nowadays.

eBay
www.ebay.co.uk

One of the most successful of Internet start-ups, eBay is the original online auction business and is worth a fortune. It's not hard to see why it's so popular, and why it has spread its operations from its California base to many other countries. The Web site offers a massive amount of products in every possible category – and that includes the antiques and collectibles section. On the UK site there are thousands of items listed clearly under categories that range from writing instruments to farm equipment, feng shui wind chimes and many other odd objects. It's fascinating for the idle browser to look at what's on offer, but absolutely essential for the collector, whether buying or selling.

Objects are listed with a brief description, the closing date of the auction, and the current highest bid. Most also have a photograph. To bid for an item you first have to register, then simply enter your price. The site will even carry out 'proxy bidding' to your pre-set upper limit (which no other bidders can see).

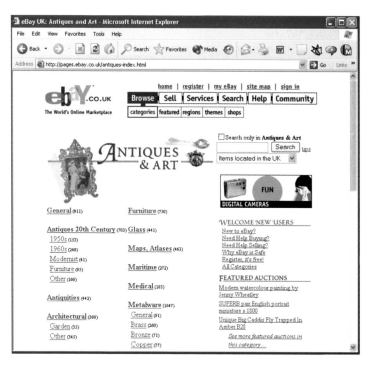

icollector
www.icollector.com

This site positions itself in an upmarket stratum of the online auction world: you are more likely to find Picasso lithographs and Georgian sideboards than wind chimes. Nor does it stick exclusively to online auctions; at least as important are the links it provides to 'real-world' auctions around the UK. These give full details of what's on sale, accompanied by many photographs. The site also heavily features comic book auctions, although there are lots of links to dealers and galleries at the more expensive end of the market. This is a clean and smartly designed site that's well worth examining if you're looking for something a little bit special.

Vintage Postcards
www.vintagepostcards.com

It's difficult to know if old postcards are antiques or collectibles. Perhaps the word 'vintage', as applied to cars, is the term that fits best. They are much sought after by an avid collecting community. This site has a well-illustrated online catalogue, covering topics from Art Nouveau to social history. It's fully searchable, and you can buy online or take part in online auctions. It's a fascinating site and well worth a browse.

● About the index
Text in italics is used for cross-references within the index (as in *see also...*). Page numbers in bold type denote the main entries for a topic.

● **Acknowledgments**
Abbreviations: t = top; b = bottom;
r = right; l = left; c = centre;
bkg = background. All cartoons
are by Chris Bramley

8	De Agostini
12	De Agostini
16tr	Lyndon Parker/De Agostini
20t	Lyndon Parker/De Agostini
24	(Beethoven) AKG
24	(Prodigy) Redferns
30b	Lyndon Parker/De Agostini
34	Lyndon Parker/De Agostini
36t	Lyndon Parker/De Agostini
38t	Lyndon Parker/De Agostini
44	Lyndon Parker
46t	Lyndon Parker/De Agostini
48tr	Lyndon Parker/De Agostini
50bl	Lyndon Parker/De Agostini
52tr	The Stock Market
54	MGM/Kobal Collection
56	MGM/Kobal Collection
58	MGM/Kobal Collection
60	NASA
62	Tony Stone Images/Olney Vasan

64	Lyndon Parker
66	Lyndon Parker/De Agostini
74	The Stock Market
75cl	The Stock Market
77	The Stock Market
78	Lyndon Parker/De Agostini
82	Lyndon Parker/De Agostini
84	Getty Images
90	Lyndon Parker/De Agostini
92	Adobe
96all	Lyndon Parker/De Agostini
97t,b	Lyndon Parker/De Agostini
99	Lyndon Parker/De Agostini
100all	Lyndon Parker/De Agostini
101	Hewlett Packard
102t	De Agostini
102b	Steve Bartholomew/De Agostini
103tl	Logitech
103cr	PMC Consumer ElectronicsLtd
104t	The Stock Market
104cr	Olitec UK
105t	US Robotics
106	Lyndon Parker/De Agostini
108	Lyndon Parker/De Agostini
109all	Seiko (courtesy)
110cr	Nokia
110bl	Psion

111tr	3Com (courtesy)
112	Canon
113t	Canon
113bl	Xircom
113br	Palm
114t	Xircom
114br	Lite On
115tl	Kensington®
115cr	Lyndon Parker/De Agostini
115b	Lyndon Parker/De Agostini
115bl	Kensington®
116	(dancers) Stockmarket
116	(speakers) Lyndon Parker/De Agostini
117all	Lyndon Parker/De Agostini
120all	©Disney Enterprises, Inc
121all	©Disney Enterprises, Inc
122	De Agostini
126	Tony Stone Images
128	De Agostini
129	De Agostini
130	Andy Teare/De Agostini
134	De Agostini
138	Image Bank
139tr	Getty One Stone
142all	De Agostini
143all	De Agostini
154	The Stock Market